MW00652754

Just a Thought

S. L. Brown

MAR 16, 2019

Cody,

Thank you for your
service and taking
time to read my thoughts.
Enjoy the read!

So happy our paths crossed
and you are on the
journey with us. April

All rights reserved.
ISBN: 978-0-692-88914-5

seans-thoughts.com

3

Acknowledgements

I have to dedicate this book to my mother Wanda, father Robert, stepmother Edwina and my wife Keziah. I don't believe I would be the man I am without the guidance, love, trust and support from these foundations to my life, my strength, my compassion and my belief in me. I am grateful for each of you and hope that I have made you all proud of the man I have become.

After my parents and wife I would hate myself if I did not thank my brothers and sisters in arms serving in the Armed Forces. A very special one to two lost brothers Air Force Master Sergeant S. Auckman and Army Specialist D. Poulin who were killed serving in Iraq and Afghanistan. It is in their memory, and others who gave their lives, that I finally publish this book. They gave their lives so the least I could do is honor and cherish mine. I salute you, the fallen, you the surviving, you the serving and you that will serve one day. Thank You.

Lastly I have to thank the friends who have shown me so much support over the years from my military brothers Hairy Sax, Huggy Bear, Moe B, Frenchie J Deverson, Uncle Ruck, Chief Flowers and so many others I can't list them all. I am honored to have served with you all.

To my hippie-witch friend Beckie who has pushed me to share my thoughts, opinions and views with the world from the very first ever thought on the social media pages. Her support has been unwavering, authentic and a downright gift. Thank You my friend.

Also, my friend April who did so much leg work from reading, commenting, helping me edit, finding proof readers, doing the research to publish and providing the cookies and coffee for our many hours of working to put this together. When I finally sit with a hard copy of this book I will owe a great deal to your hard work over these past few months. Thank You as well my friend.

Speaking of proof readers I want to thank Angel, Jim, Norma and Darlene who took time to read parts of my book, gave me valuable feedback without knowing who the author was or what the book was about. April said she knew the perfect people to read it and she was right. I am forever grateful for your time and energy. Thank you.

The last thing I want to acknowledge is you the reader. You did not have to buy, rent, check-out, download, share or whatever this book but you chose to do one of those. I am humbled and thankful that you are taking a brief journey with me. Now on you go to your journey.

Introduction

Everyone one of us has a history. We all possess an insight that only each individual can call his/her own based on the life that he/she has lived. It is in that which brings this book to the world. OK, technically the war in Afghanistan brought this book to life. Let me explain. Back in 2010 while deployed to Baghram Airfield in Afghanistan I started to write random thoughts I was having based on a myriad of goings on in the world, my mind, my family and friends lives or just because it hit my brain. This book contains those thoughts from my social media page in the order as they came to me. You'll take a journey with me through the early days where messages had limitations on post length to the time where length no longer mattered and my thoughts were, well, a bit more wordy.

Now, let me be clear. These thoughts are a road from A to B but they are not the end all to be all nor are they are to be the answer to the world's problems. They are, however, thoughts that should make you, well, think. As I re-read them I am fascinated by not only the growth I have had over the years but also the messages that have impacted me over the same time frame. Now, as I put this book together in 2017 I look to share that growth, that passion, that new moment with you. As the reader, yes, you right there, my hope is that within these words you too find your own personal growth. Actually, that is a lie, I simply want to make you think. Think of something you might not have thought of before, or if you have, maybe what I have said will help solidify what you already think. No matter the case, I hope you enjoy the journey of my musings, my ramblings and, well, my thoughts.

Before you go on your own adventure with my words I must make a few disclaimers or, at the very least, explain a couple things about what you might see as you read along. These thoughts are written as they were posted on my social media site. They have not been altered with the exception of fixing the grammatical errors. Some will be full on stand-alone thoughts while others may leave you wondering what it means to you. Then there are the ones, if we are lucky, that will make you think long and hard about your life, your journey through it and where you might be headed. The last point, before I let you get to reading, is that there will be pictures that I have taken over the years on my cellphone. These pictures are mental breaks that I invite you to simply explore. What you find or don't find in them will be totally up to you, your interpretation and your history. Just remember there are no wrong reactions to these images. Now, get in there and enjoy the journey. I'll see you on the other side.

Military Day Thought: Whether you believe in war or not, support the government or protest its positions, if you are an activist or a pacifist, if you care for your family, have the ability to care for them, have kids who can go to college, have toys, are free to laugh and grow, thank a Soldier, Sailor, Airman, Marine and Guardsman for that freedom. Thank You all who serve or served and their families.
May 31, 2010

2nd Military Thought: Thank You to the men and women of the armed forces who sacrifice so much for so little. Thank You to the families of those who serve who sacrifice even more to keep kids going without a parent. Most importantly Thank You to all those who spilled blood and gave their lives for my freedom.
May 31, 2010

Be like you were when you were a kid. Don't be afraid to make your dreams big, your adventures grand and your ideas out of this world. Do not trap yourself with the mental cages we put on our imaginations. Dreams fail when we fail to dream. We fail when we stop trying to have the adventures in life. Be a child for a day, live, laugh and enjoy!
June 8, 2010

As the morning starts flush away the bad dreams, shake off the negative energy and remove the doubtful coat that surrounds you as you leave for the day. Feel the warmth of the sun, the strength of the clouds or cleansing nature of the rain. Let whatever the day brings energize you to be stronger and better than the day before.
June 8, 2010

Sometimes we wake up and don't want to do anything, we don't have the energy, the effort or the desire to get going. Allow yourself a day to do nothing and don't feel bad about it. Be free enough to do nothing. Just don't let it become the only thing you do day after day. Sometimes it's OK to relax. Pick a day to relax and be happy.
June 9, 2010

A friend isn't the one who says you look good; they tell you when you look bad. A friend doesn't tell you how smart you are; they tell you when you're being a dumbass. A friend doesn't tell you what you want to hear; they say what you NEED to hear like it or not. A friend won't stand by you as you spiral out of control; they will stand in front of you and try to stop the downfall. What kind of friend are you?
June 10, 2010

Do not expect others to know what you are thinking. Do not expect others to speak for you. Do not expect others to be your voice. Only you can speak what is on your mind. Only you can tell people how you feel. Only you can use your voice. When we do not speak for ourselves we are slaves to others' will. Speak for yourself!
June 12, 2010

Walking in the sunshine, checking the birds in flight, listening to the world around me. Then I realize how little and insignificant we as people really are on a cosmic and global scale.
June 15, 2010

What should you do when a place is hit with a tornado or hurricane? Slap yourself because your dumb butt shouldn't have been in any place that has them in the first place.
June 16, 2010

When one cheats to gain success the taste is bitter. When one is dishonest in the pursuit of getting ahead the ground is not solid. When one undermines others to build their own bridge to success the bridge is shaky. It is easy to lose what is gained without strong foundation. Use integrity, honesty and humility to gain success that way no one can take it from you.
June 16, 2010

We can never really understand the status of our relationships if we never take a step back and define them in our world. Many of our relationships, both personal and professional, are unhealthy for us; yet, we continue to hang onto them. Do not feed something that does not make you a better person. One-sided relationships are unhealthy to your mental and physical growth. Is it time to clean your closet?
June 24, 2010

4th of July Thought: Always remember, the USA was born on the backs of those who refused to live under others rule. Paid with blood of those who would give their all in defense of Freedom. To the Native Americans, the Colonists, The Confederates, The Union, Blacks, Whites, Asians, Hispanics, Africans, Indians and all the other races that make up this great Nation, Happy B-Day to you United States of America!
July 4, 2010

Never assume that what you see is what you know. Acting on an assumption or forming an opinion on it can and will often lead you to misguided notions. Remember, the first thought isn't always the right thought. Take care to not let misguided words trap you in a sticky situation.
July 9, 2010

Never allow others ideas, choices and beliefs to make you not believe in yourself. If you do not believe in yourself no one else can truly believe in you. Truth starts inside, fight starts inside and belief comes from your core. Believe in you and trust in your choices but be smart enough to see the error in your ways and to not make them again.
July 11, 2010

Mother Nature shows us the best way to make a change in our lives. Never be like an earthquake, for its sudden abruptness and destruction only rips apart. Don't be the hurricane, for its waters may cleanse, its winds will remove all that you hold dear. Instead, be the river that transforms the land over time with constant pressure and flow. It takes its time and does it with purpose and resolve. Be the river.

July 12, 2010

Do not be rigid when embarking on your journey with others. Instead let the world bend you, let it stretch you, let it twist you til you can't take any more. Allow it to do all those things but NEVER let it break you. Flexibility is the key to success. Adaptability is the key to getting through the hard times. Never be the rigid one!

July 20, 2010

It matters not that you have identified a change in you that needs to be made. It matters not that you have made the change for better or for worse. What matters is that you understand the purpose of the change and that you have done it solely for yourself to better yourself. Change done for others is change that will be undone by others. Change for YOU!

July 28, 2010

Always remember that when times are roughest and darkest it is when our true light shines brightest. No matter the issue, no matter the fight and no matter the opposition the strength you have will always be enough to come out on top and better for it. We do not get stronger from the praises and trophies we get in life. Instead, we get stronger from the times we are knocked down and counted out.

July 30, 2010

Sunday is for church but I don't go to church. Sunday is for doing some yard work but I am at a place where the yard houses the prisoners. Sunday is for eating with your family but here my family are all wearing uniforms. Sunday is a day of rest, relaxation and recharging but for me Sunday is a day of 4 hours of sleep, meetings, running around and pushing through that "low battery" light, and "That's what I love about Sunday."
Aug 8, 2010

Do not neglect the "Prizes" in your life. Do not make things that are expendable into prizes and do not make things that are prizes expendable. A car can be replaced no matter how much you paid for it. However, trust, love and friendship cannot be replaced no matter how many new relationships you create. Keep your "prizes" dust free and a looking new like a million dollar antique collection. What's your Prize?
Aug 19, 2010

Take a stroll down memory lane and allow yourself to relive some of the landmarks of your mind. Fully remember the experience, the weather, the feelings, the air, the taste, the touch and all the other senses you can feel. Allow yourself to enjoy it and if you feel compelled, share the great experience with someone. Recharge your happiness.
August 22, 2010

Never allow yourself to react when you are hurt, frustrated, or angry. Instead, allow yourself a moment to cool off so you can think clearly. Speaking or acting when angry can cause infinitely more damage than you intend to spark. Do not let an emotion destroy what you have created.
August 29, 2010

One can only mend what is broken by first proving they themselves can be trusted. What is destroyed with lies can never be rebuilt until the lies are cleansed from the soul. Afterthought recognition does not fix the underlying lies. Honesty starts and ends with oneself. Truth can only be obtained when truth is sought for oneself.
Sept 7, 2010

No matter how bad your day is going taking a real good Deuce always makes you feel soooooooooooooooooo much better.
Sept 13, 2010

At the very moment you feel your lowest, you feel life is about to break and you feel like you can't take any more pressure. STAND UP. Stand up to your doubt, to your pain, to your fear of failure. The only thing that can stop you from success is yourself. Every pain has a cure, every hurdle has a victor and every trap has an escape. Find the power in yourself to be better than your doubt.
Sept 17, 2010

To take a life is tragic. To take your own life is a tragedy unequal to any other tragedy. Life in its whole is painful yet wonderful. It is rough yet smooth. It is harsh yet rewarding. One can never shine bright as a star if one never understands that the star shines from within. No tragedy can ever be explained. Do not allow yourself to be the next tragedy
Oct 8, 2010

I never promise a future because it is not within my grasp to deliver. Instead, I promise to be true to myself as it is the only honesty I can give to those who care enough to hope for my safety and success in life.
Oct 12, 2010

As I embark on this journey with my new brothers and sisters in arms I want you all to remember we serve so you can be free, we serve so others can grow and we serve to protect the weak. If you respect what I do then the next time you see a Veteran, in uniform or not... THANK THEM. I'll miss you all until I return.
Oct 18, 2010

Many people talk about (their) God's way of love and what we as men should do. Many boast loudly of how others should make the world better. Many of those people have never stood up for someone who doesn't believe what they believe, feel what the feel nor celebrate what they celebrate. If you wish to make the world better start with your own hypocrisy.
Oct 25, 2010

Never allow another person's hate to taint your view of the world. Spend more time finding the beauty in yourself, your friends, your family and your world and then spread that to the rest of the world. No one has ever been scared to go into the light, but the darkness is something else. Be the positive that others wish you weren't.
Oct 27, 2010

In every challenge there are many solutions. The key is to find the solution that will allow you to look at yourself in the mirror. Sometimes the easiest answer is the worst choice while the most difficult answer can be the most rewarding. Choose your solutions with great care, for it may be the biggest choice of your life.
Oct 30, 2010

On a day of tricking and treating I am left with the idea that I was tricked into believing I couldn't love anyone as much as I do myself. However, I was treated to the fact that I love you infinitely more than I could ever love myself or anyone else. I love you dear.
Oct 31, 2010

You are different today than you were yesterday. You have grown and learned and become (hopefully) a better you. You may not be who you were but remember you are always who you have been. Be you, be at peace, be happy.
Nov 5, 2010

Sometimes I wish to shoot people for being absolutely stupid and not understanding the basic human functions that a retarded monkey would be able to understand. However, as a civilized person I'll just walk away and curse their parents for not using protection.
Nov 11, 2010

On this Veteran's Day I want to thank all the wives, husbands, daughters, sons, parents and siblings of those who are serving or have served. The hardest job in the Military is a Military spouse. The families we leave behind keep us strong, in great spirits, and focused on getting home to our loved ones. Thank You for being strong for us.
Nov 11, 2010

A Veteran is nothing more than a warrior without having a family and friends to fight for at home. I am a hero because you are worth fighting for and dying for. Thank You for being the wife of a Sailor/Airman and sacrificing so much in order to support me. I love you, cherish you and am forever grateful. Happy Veteran's Day Wife!
Nov 11, 2010

A Fallen Hero ceremony is what we do when a warrior dies here in the war. In the past nine days there have been 9 of them. I did my first yesterday and will be doing 3 more tomorrow sometime. Some Soldiers, Sailors, Airmen and Marines never make it back. How much have you paid for your freedom?
November 14, 2010

Do not allow the negative words that you say become the reality of the things that you do. If you wish to no longer do something or be something then choose not to be it. It starts with your thoughts, then your choice of words and then your actions. Confidence in yourself is the only way to defeat your self-destruction.
November 24, 2010

Turkey Day Thought: Be not Thankful for the things that you have in your life. Instead, be Thankful for the lives you have touched and made better, for within it you have gained the best things in life that is trust, faith, hope and love. Then, be Thankful for those in your life that have made you better. Happy Thanksgiving!
November 25, 2010

Check yourself. If you are over the age of 30 and you don't have any laugh lines then I wonder, "What the hell are you doing?" We spend too much of our life worried about losses that aren't, loves that weren't and failures that couldn't succeed. Live free, love completely and laugh till your belly explodes.
Nov 28, 2010

Do not allow success in life to cloud your view on you. Do not let your eyes tell you a story your brain knows not to be true. Stand, enjoy, learn and grow but never get seduced by the sexy vision you believe you see. Truth requires no seduction.
Dec 2, 2010

Everyone is changing their Facebook profile pictures to cartoons to "fight child abuse". This is a nice gesture but I wonder how many of the millions of Facebook posters would actually call and help a child being abused? How many would get "involved" or how many just wanted to take a trip back to their childhood and talk about cartoons? I wonder.

Dec 4, 2010

We are sheep as people. One day ago Facebook was covered in cartoon characters for "the kids". Today, all back to normal cause of "pedophiles" allegedly starting the movement. Don't back something just because it "sounds" good. Before you put your name on anything be willing to risk your name to whatever it is. Do not blindly follow anything.

Dec 6, 2010

Cherish those in your life who are strong enough to be truthful with you no matter the consequences. It is a rare relationship that is often overlooked and underappreciated. When you lose it you will find that you are crippled both physically and mentally by the loss. Be careful of the bridges you burn for it may be the very foundation that is keeping you up.

Dec 14, 2010

As we all wake up tomorrow and spend Christmas without families, take a moment and say a prayer for all those who can't be with their families and those families who have lost a loved one over the years. My prayers go out to all those service members overseas for a safe return home to their loved ones and to those who may be spending their first Christmas without them.

Dec 24, 2010

You are never the first to walk a path, however, it is the first time YOU have walked it. Keep your eyes, ears and mind open to the things that others missed before you. Then you can share a new perspective on an old story. Learn from being brave enough to see things differently.
Jan 4, 2011

Be mindful of the effect you have on others be it positive or negative. Somewhere someone is depending on you to keep them grounded and be "strength" when they can't find it. Take care to understand when someone needs you. Be the strength but not a crutch. Who picks you up?
Jan 8, 2011

Do not convince yourself of something untrue even if it is to protect your heart. The truth always lies somewhere between what you think, what you believe, what you feel and what you know. Being able to unmask your own veils is a sign of true wisdom.
Feb 2, 2011

V-Day Thought: Take the time to recall why you fell in love in the first place, take time to remember the first kiss, the first touch and the first "time". Remember the pain and struggles make you stronger in love. Never forget that you swore to protect that person. Take time to show them you truly LOVE them. Happy V-Day friends.
Feb 14, 2011

You can only grow if you are willing to take a chance. But if you stay on the shore you will never learn to swim; if you stay on the ground you will never learn to fly; and if you stay in the box you will never learn to grow. Be willing to be better than you are.

Feb 20, 2011

Be careful of what you are willing to toss out into the wind be it property, words, thoughts or relationships. You never know what "property" could be valuable, what "words" could create a masterpiece, what "thoughts" could be another's salvation and what "relationships" could be The One. A diamond does not look like a diamond to start and a Rose grows from Poo. Be Careful of what you toss away!

Feb 22, 2011

Take a moment to understand what you have in front of you. Take the time to cherish the laughter of your kids, the look in the eye of your love and the undying faith of your family. Be strong in the strength that others have put in you.

Feb 24, 2011

What is Love? Love is knowing that when you are down in the dumps there is someone to stand up to pick you up, Being Strong when they are weak and believing that you can make it through the horrible times even when your mate isn't so sure. Love is COMMITMENT!

Feb 26, 2011

As my Sunday winds to a close, another week down, and a day closer to going home I am left to wonder how much will have changed. Every soldier I see go on a plane, every rocket that hits my area, every person I see leave has all changed me. What kind of man will I be? One wonders what a war really does to a person's perspective. Growth or Destruction?
Feb 27, 2011

One cannot control the path of a tornado no more than we can control the paths of the people in our lives. Some will wish to stay, some wish to go, some wish to lift you and some break you down. How you deal with the aftermath is what will define you when it is all said and done. Love You!
March 8, 2011

Everything we have been through in life has created who we are today Everything we are today will create who we will be in the future; and thus we are who we are in all of our being. BE YOU!
March 27, 2011

A life is precious. It can be gone in a second. I have seen death, looked at its ugliness and had to carry on. Today I am without strength and without understanding of the purpose of life as it is. My backbone has left me to fend for myself. I shall stand again but today I am weaker by this precious life. Wow.
March 28, 2011

Even the strong have to lean on someone. No one can be the wall all the time. We must allow ourselves the humility of allowing others to be there for you. Needing others is not a sign of weakness but a true sign of "Real" Strength.
March 31, 2011

Fallen Thought: Today SPC Dennis Poulin from the 181 Yankee Division, Camp Wright Asadabad, gave his life. Born in 1985 this young man added to the bright red color of the American Flag. My heart is broken at the memory of carrying this soldier on a plane to the place he would stop breathing. I salute SPC Poulin. "Gone but not forgotten".
Apr 1, 2011

Hindsight always makes something from the past better than it was when it was our present. When nostalgia passes one will be left feeling emptier than before they relit the past. In the end it is those who will find you in the dark and want to lead you to the light no matter what you have done that really matter to your heart and mind. Never throw away a coal for a fake diamond.
Apr 8, 2011

We all lose our way, we all make mistakes and we all have failed someone else and even our self. Be brave enough to fight for what you have and for what you might lose. Be passionate enough to care more about your loved ones than what happened on your favorite show. Most of all forgive, forget and re-forge stronger and better. Live!
April 11, 2011

Wishing to be forever young is the same as saying I never want to grow up. The past has made us, the present is building us and the future will showcase our personal greatness. Never long for what you once were, instead long for what you will be. We Are Growth!
April 13, 2011

People say "I love you" all the time. However, if they don't believe in you during the times you stop believing in you then how much could they have loved you in the first place? A spouse, a friend, a family member who really "loves" will have faith in your ability to see past your own faults and failures and will be there no matter how much you say you don't need them. Love is Believing!
April 15, 2011

To be taught a lesson in life one must first be open to opinion that is different than their own. We are given opportunities to show who we really are at every turn but if we do not grab a hold of them they will only wither away and die. Be strong in your convictions. Be Strong enough to be able to change those very convictions when life has shown you a better way. Evolve a better YOU!
April 18, 2011

If you approach life with a negative outlook you will begin to become negative without knowing it. Positivity and believing in others may open you up for being hurt but not going with those will leave you empty. Living without faith is not living at all. Allow yourself to be free to Live, Love and Laugh.
April 21, 2011

Don't wait for a holiday to be the person you would like to be. Don't wait for tomorrow or a better time in your life either. Instead, decide today to be the person you want the world to see. Be genuine, be natural, be caring, be loving but most of all BE REAL.
April 23, 2011

Sometimes you have to be subtle with the truth and sometimes you have to be downright blunt about it. The hard part is knowing when you should be open and honest about what you feel or know. Relationships and friendships all thrive on the ability for the other person to believe in you and your word.
May 5, 2011

Mom's Day Thought: Understand that a mom is unique. She is a "love" force that holds a family together. She is a soft hand to calm a nerve, fragile and strong, capable of compassion and generosity. She is more than we can ever understand. Cherish her while she is with you. I wish a Happy Mother's Day to my wife Keziah, mothers Wanda, Edwina, Kathy and a special "Missing you" to Cheryl Woodside up in heaven watching over us.
May 8, 2011

As my journey back to war continues I am left with the notion of mortality. We have promised to do so much in our lives to friends, loved ones and ourselves yet we never do it. Take the time to remember why you were in love, the promises you made yourself and the joys you wish to share with others. Live b4 you die.
May 11, 2011

When trying to walk out of darkness do not allow yourself to be fooled by false lights. An old candle may light an old flame to help you find your way, however, remember it was an old candle for a reason. Follow the light that has always been there, for it will always show you the way no other candle could. BELIEVE!
May 14, 2011

There are many sides to each of us. Allow people to see the softer side of you more than the hard side. Being aware of others' emotional needs will make you a stronger and better mate, lover and friend. Look into yourself and see the "real" you that people would love to know. BE FREE.
May 15, 2011

When you wake up in the morning try your best to spread a smile to someone you love or care about. Send a simple poem, a note saying how much you love them or just a good morning passionate kiss. Do not take for granted that they know you care. Instead, take for granted that they need to be reminded you do. BE SPONTANEOUS WITH LOVE!
May 16, 2011

Life can feel helpless but being down on one knee doesn't mean you are down. Being on both knees doesn't mean you are down. Only when you "lay down" and stop trying to stand are you truly down. As long as you are willing to fight to stand then anything is possible. The world may beat you down but never let it knock you out. STAND AND DELIVER!
May 17, 2011

A wife can make you angry. She can hurt you more than any other person in the world. She can be hard and over critical. She can be a pain in the butt. Yes, all those things, but she will always make you happy again. Make you happier than ever before, be soft and sympathetic and make you feel the greatest love ever made. A wife is someone who knows how to make you feel special. Thank You, wife!

May 18, 2011

Give a smile and get a smile back. Give praise and get a joyful response. Give your time and get forever grateful. Give Love and get Love back 10 fold. BUT if you GIVE UP you will without a doubt get NOTHING back. Start to give!

May 19, 2011

The world has no memory. We live, we die and it carries on. Waves wash away memories, wind carries away scents and traces of our presence, and earth covers and conceals all that remains. When dealing with past pains be like the world and wash away the pain, whisk away the sour smell and cover up its remains. Start over like the sands of a beach after a wave. FORGIVE!
May 20, 2011

One can only follow their dreams if they are willing to take the leap of faith off the highest cliff the doubters can build. Believe in yourself enough to stand in the midst of ridicule, laughter and doubt and say "I WILL SUCCEED. "To reach for a star you must be willing to fly in space.
May 23, 2011

Memorial Thought: We put our lives on the line for those who cannot. We have died alone in places most cannot spell or even say. Our enemies have no honor yet we refuse to fight without it. We are Soldiers, Sailors, Airmen and Marines both past and present. We bow our heads for those who made the RED in the flag a little brighter with the ultimate sacrifice. THANK YOU!
May 23, 2011

We say I love you and I'll stand by you till death does us part. One can be forever in your eyes in good times. However, REAL one's will love you, stand by you and be forever in your eyes when things are rocky, stormy and impossible. True testament to Love is what you do when you aren't your best or nicest. Love grows stronger from hard times not good times. Be strong, stand tall and love them through the hard times. IT IS WORTH IT!
May 24, 2011

Life is only meaningful if you put meaning to it. What you value and what is truly worth giving everything up for is what puts the price on your life. Do not sell your life short by giving value to things that aren't worth it. Know the worth of your friends and family but most of all know your worth. Live life to its most meaningful.
May 26, 2011

In order to elevate your mind you must first let go of preconceived notions of what you know and think you know. True knowledge comes to those who are strong enough to be wrong yet willing to believe they are right when conviction is needed. Being open to "possibilities" will strengthen your stance the right way.
May 27, 2011

When you fall on your face do not worry about the scrapes, cuts and bruises you may have from it. Instead stand up and be proud of the scars that were created from the lesson life has taught you. The scars we gain are the tough lessons in life we have learned. Be proud of your failures but learn from them first.
May 28, 2011

"Air Force Master Sergeant Steve Auckman (Iraq Sep 2003) and Army Specialist Dennis Poulin (Afghanistan April 2011)": Memorial Day is not another faceless holiday. It is a close to home homage to our fallen brothers and sisters who never made it home. My heart beats stronger because they watch over me as I fight for our freedom. Happy Memorial Day, my fallen Brothers and Sisters. Heaven needs great defenders.
May 30, 2011

A child is not an extension of his or her parents. Instead, a child is a beginning of something completely new. Do not put your bias, your failures and your hopes for self on their shoulders. Instead, mold them to stand on their own and they will reward you with being brave enough to be themselves. BE A PARENT!
June 1, 2011

Do not take for granted the gestures others make for you no matter how small they may seem. A simple thank you, a smile or a show of real enjoyment or appreciation can be the world to someone. When you receive something from the heart be kind enough to return the favor and be Thankful and Grateful. RECIPROCATE!
June 3, 2011

Pour your heart and soul into a dream and that dream has its greatest chance to grow. Never allow weeds (outside negatives) to overtake the potential of your dream's success. Believe in yourself enough to see your dreams come true. BELIEVE!
June 4, 2011

When a wave hits a beach it is the culmination of a journey that started thousands of miles earlier. In order for it to be successful it had to stay its course and no matter the obstacle it will reach the beach. The "Wave" is your journey and the "Beach" is your goals/dreams. Let nothing stand in the way of you reaching the shores of your destiny.
June 5, 2011

(Forrest Gump style): We are like a toilet bowl. Be mindful to keep yourself clean and free of a lot of waste. If you do not flush the crap out you can back up and spill shit all over your world. So flush all the drama away and use bleach every once in awhile :)
June 6, 2011

When we make excuses for others we only cripple them and ourselves. In today's society we make excuses for kids learning and attention issues, parents' inabilities to actually "parent", the government's lack of integrity and a myriad of other things. In order to fix it you must first be accountable for the person in the mirror. Truth starts with YOU!
June 7, 2011

People have spent a lifetime searching for their very own Atlantis. Finding a perfect world created by someone else does not make it anymore perfect for you, as would be *your* life for your children. Your perfect world can only be found in you and that which you hold dear to you.
June 8, 2011

Do not let disappointment in others cloud your ability to forgive and forget. Be wise enough to see each situation as its own thing and deal accordingly. If you are hurt, be honest. If you feel wronged, speak up and allow the other person a chance to prove you may have been wrong or proven right.
June 10, 2011

Before you lay your head to sleep think of those who would give their lives for you. When you wake up, before you curse the alarm, sigh for the missing hours you wish you had, or just scream from having to go to work again, take a minute to just feel the love that others from husbands, wives, kids, parents, siblings and friends give you every day. Start and end your day with LOVE.
June 11, 2011

Be patient with life. No matter how much you try and do what you think is "the right thing" you may not get the result you wish right away. Do not push what can't be pushed and do not rush what can't be rushed. Instead allow yourself to see the small gains your work has garnered. In the end you will feel better about the outcome be it negative or positive. BE PATIENT!
June 12, 2011

Fail to live an honest life internally you will fail to "live" life. A lie will eat at your soul. Contempt directed at others can often be found rooted deep inside of your own heart as self-contempt. Find the root of your pain and find the peace to be able to live an honest life. You cannot be truthful to others until you first tell yourself the truth. BE THE TRUTH!
June 13, 2011

Life doesn't always give us what we really want. In fact, it can feel like it is kicking the living crap out of us. It is those times we find our true strength within ourselves. The only time hope is lost is when we give up on our dreams. When you are weak, lean on your friends to help give you strength and then kick life's ass. BELIEVE!
June 15, 2011

One can only reach enlightenment if one is open to the possibilities of each situation they find themselves in. Do not be so quick to dismiss a possibility because "I won't do that" or "I don't do that" or something similar. Seeing things from different perspectives allows you to make a truly informed choice. Enlighten yourself enough to be open to possibilities.
June 16, 2011

Do not say or post things on Facebook about people that you would not, could not or should not say to them in person. You cannot un-shoot a bullet nor can you just "delete" a comment. Posting things in anger or annoyance can and often will shoot you in the butt. Do not do something you wouldn't do if the computer/phone wasn't protecting you. THINK!
June 17, 2011

Father's Day Thought: Fathers teach determination, respect, self-respect and discipline. We are the muscle behind the Mother's caring grace. We beat the monsters under the bed and scare the boogieman. We are airplanes and horses and the one that every child wishes to impress. Most importantly we stand by our spouses in the honor of raising our children. Happy Father's Day to all the Fathers out there.
June 18, 2011

In order to succeed you need a few things. 1) Desire to do what it takes to make it happen. 2) Surround yourself with people who will give you "REAL" advice and support. 3) Make "Failure" an absolute option. In fact embrace that you are willing to fail. 4) Know what "SUCCESS" means to you and go get it. BE SUCCESSFUL!
June 20, 2011

Being a friend means telling someone how to succeed no matter what it does to you. Giving them the guidance to be their very best even if it means you are no longer part of it. A true friend wants you to be your best and will always guide you to that very goal. What Kind of Friend Are You?

June 21, 2011

Before you take any action you must first ask yourself a couple of things. 1) Am I prepared for "if it goes wrong"? 2) Is this the best choice for me? 3) How will it affect me and others? 4) Is it worth the ramifications and can I live with the consequences. Do not do something you will regret later if it comes to light. If you do it OWN IT and ACCEPT all that comes with it.

June 22, 2011

All people will let you down at some point but only the great few will pick you back up when they do. Be mindful of your expectations that others do not know about. A person cannot live up to or exceed what is not known to them. Share your opinion and wants openly and honestly and in that you may find what you are really looking for in life.

June 23, 2011

Take notice of how much negative you spread in your world from complaints about work, the weather, money, the dogs or a myriad of other things. This weekend take a moment to enjoy the sunrise, sunset, birds singing, a glass of ice tea in the shade while the kids play or cuddle up & enjoy a movie with a love. Make the day about nothing but one positive action after another. BE POSITIVE!
June 24, 2011

A baby will laugh hysterically at a peak-a-boo. A child will squeal with excitement from being chased and threatened to be tickled. Kids find enjoyment in the simple fun pleasures of life. Adults forget what "true" joy is all about. Laugh like an infant, squeal like a happy child and most importantly stop "acting" grown up all the time. BE OLD ENOUGH TO BE A KID!
June 25, 2011

We say we will stand by someone through thick and thin (ride or die, if you will). In this, we show our support for them, but what happens when it is really needed? Will you stand by them when they are truly lost? Pick them up and show them the way when you are exhausted yourself? To be "there," means that when the crap hits the fan you are also there covered in shit helping your friend get out of it.

June 26, 2011

The hardest thing to do is to pick up the mirror and hold it long enough to see yourself. Get past the self-portrait and see how you can be a better person within. Share your love and your wisdom like the people of times past where our children had been taught by example and by all adults. LET'S GO BACK!

June 27, 2011

If you approach a situation, be it large or small, with a negative thought process you will never truly enjoy the outcome. However, if you use a positive process you can truly enjoy your successes and handle the failures much better. Do not lose faith in yourself, your friends or your fellow man/woman. BELIEVE IN THE POSSIBLE!
June 28, 2011

Wisdom comes from understanding that pain will make you stronger. Every tear your eye releases is a new lesson to be embraced and shared. If you allow pain and sadness the chance to grow properly they will turn into Warmth and Happiness. A wise person knows the heart beats strong because it gets highs and lows to work it out. Allow yourself to "feel" what you feel and move forward as a person.
June 29, 2011

To cultivate a relationship with a friend, relative, love or even your God of choice you must first remove the term "I" out of it. Replace it with "we," as you have to know what you and that person can do to grow together. When you care more about the two than the "you" then your relationship can grow and prosper. Build on a great foundation of trust and dependability, not on selfishness and I-ism's.
June 30, 2011

I remember when I was afraid to say "Damn" in front of my parents. Kids now curse and have provocative photos of them on FB while being friends with their parents. When we played till the streetlights came on. When kids STFU when grown folks were talking. When we sat and ate everything cooked by our mother/father. Sean's thought-what happened to the Family?
July 1, 2011

Fear can be both good and bad. It can keep you cautious and prevent you from doing something stupid. That's good fear. However, Fear to let go of the past, the pains or your own misjudgments can keep you from seeing something that could make you a better person. Fear of letting people into your world will leave you bitter and hurtful. Take time to beat your fears.
July 2, 2011

Make sacrifices for those you love but never sacrifice who you "are" for anyone. When it is all said and done you must like the person in the mirror 100%. A child brings a great joy to your life and depends on your love and guidance. However, the title of Mother or Father should not replace who you are as a person instead it should add to it/you. KNOW WHO YOU ARE!
July 3, 2011

July 4th Thought: I am a Warrior in the US Military. I've wrote a check with "...and up to my life" to the people of the US of A. I will not hide behind my failures nor brag about my successes. I will do my job for those who need me to stand for them and ask for nothing in return but fair treatment. I salute those who are away from loved ones & the families who are missing loved ones. MY CHECK 4 YOUR INDEPENDENCE!
July 4, 2011

Do not let ambitions of success cloud the journey on the path to it. If the only thing you are fighting for is more money, items, bigger houses, more cars etc. etc. then once you obtain those things you won't be satisfied. You can fill the empty hole inside all you want but it will never be filled. Instead enjoy the small victories and the benefits that come with them then you can enjoy success.
July 5, 2011

As I leave Afghanistan, I want to say I am humbled by the sacrifices so many make under extreme situations both in war and at home. I thank members of the 181 INF, who risked their lives to protect my Navy Brethren, and all the men and women I served with over here. Mostly thanks to my wife, family and friends who are the reason I am still here today. HOMEWARD BOUND!
July 6, 2011

People today talk too much. We say we are going to do this, or we are going to do that. Then we do something different. We change stances with the wind and we rarely can defend our own positions outside of what the news tells us. Let us stop following others and actually have a position in life. If you miss someone, show it. If you love them, show it. If you believe in something, SHOW IT.
July 7, 2011

Form an opinion based on your sound judgment and facts. Do not allow a bias from media outlets to guide you in a predetermined direction. Too many times we, as people, stand tall and loud for something we neither understand nor believe in completely. Knowledge can keep you from becoming a fool.

July 8, 2011

A friend told me this: When an old man who had been married 50 years was asked, how did he do it. He simply replied: The key is to never fall out of Love at the same time. Sean's Thought: Be strong enough to hold the one you love up long enough so they can do it themselves. Love is not a constant it is ever changing. Understand Love and a relationship can survive anything.

July 11, 2011

If you conquer a journey that seemed daunting and impossible while in it you will feel a true sense of accomplishment. Never let overwhelming odds, obstacles or hurdles keep you from completing what is in your heart to finish. One journey has ended and thus a new one has begun. Home Here I come!

July 12, 2011

"Potential" can only be met if you are willing to introduce yourself to "Hard Work" and "Dedication". Many older people are left with the "I could have done" and the "I should've had this or that but..." type memories that I am sure they regret in old age. It is never too late to take "potential" and turn it into "actuality". Discover something GRAND today: Discover You!

July 17, 2011

It is time to put down the "Words with Friends", the Farmvilles and Youvilles, the books and magazines. It is time to turn off the reality shows, cooking shows and sports shows. Get your kids and spouses from in front of the TV. It is time to bring back family conversation and quality time. Play with your kids and show your spouse they are the most important things in the world.
July 19, 2011

We are all lost at some point in our various relationships and in life. The key to finding our way out is to have faith in your mind, believe in your heart and listen to those who "actually" have your best interest at heart. Nothing is ever destroyed as long as you believe you can fix it and are willing to work hard to do so.
July 19, 2011

The hardest battle anyone can face is the battle within themselves. The battle against their desires, self-doubt, overvalued sense of self and their fears. We can't win that battle on our own. Instead, we must surround ourselves with those who not only care for our best but are capable of holding us up when we can't do it. Never battle alone. Trust in those who really love you and will stand with you.
July 21, 2011

If you cannot say what you think to the person you are talking about then you probably shouldn't say it to someone else about them. Be brave enough to speak your mind honestly and openly to those who need to hear it. Do not hide behind secret conversations and open-ended Facebook quotes. Stand by your thoughts and opinions not behind computer screens and friends.
July 22, 2011

Do not let your emotions or hurt feelings get in the way of listening and understanding how someone else feels. Your reaction could close the door to communication and make something small much worse. Take a step back if you have to but listen to them first and express why you are/were hurt. Proper communication can save many relationships.

July 25, 2011

To parent means to teach, guide, educate and mold for the future. Unfortunately, many have failed not only themselves but also their kids. Try teaching our young girls how to be women and our young boys how to be men. Our society continues to flush down the crapper as more and more young adults fail to have integrity, self-respect and humility. What a Shame!

July 26, 2011

Take the time to self-reflect on the mental and physical image you show the world. You may think you're a great mom, husband, best(est) friend ever etc. but the reality is something completely different. Do not convince yourself of a truth that does not exist. We are all 3 people: how we see ourselves, how people see us and how we really are. Get to know all of them. You might be amazed.
July 27, 2011

Commitment is staying in the fire when it is too hot to stand, when you may be the only one standing in it, when you feel like there isn't any hope of getting out but you still believe it will get cooler, you won't always be alone and you will make it out of the struggles. Be willing to stand for what you have created through all cost.
July 31, 2011

A mountain isn't carved in a day it is etched out over time. Be mindful that your actions today will often be reflected over the course of time. You never know how your actions will affect the universe as a whole. Speak with honesty, act with good intentions and remain humble in your place in the world. Maybe your mountain will be one to be proud of.
Aug 1, 2011

One can never stop the hands of time. Our lives will end when they are destined to end no matter what we do. What time cannot take away is the impact we have on others and the memory we leave within their minds and hearts. Your legacy isn't about the money and property you have but the value of your word and your person in the eyes of the one's who loved you most. What will your legacy be?

Aug 3, 2011

There is only one thing in the world we have an excess of. We cannot waste it if we tried. It will not diminish if we use it nor expire if we don't. It is the one thing if given honestly can brighten a day, change a mood, and make you feel safe, warm and secure. If given dishonestly, it can ruin a person's faith, destroy friendships, and relationships. Go into your National Reserve and share a little LOVE today.

Aug 4, 2011

"Family" does not mean, "owe you something". We spend more time taking advantage of those closest to us than we do protecting and building them up. Family is supposed to make you stronger, make you feel safe and be a sanctuary for your mental and physical well-being. They are not your babysitters, financiers or your dumping points. Stand with them, not on their backs, and you may get more out of a better relationship with them.

Aug 5, 2011

B-Day Thought: A year of a life will only be worth it if you have a great outlook, great loves, great friends and amazing support. As I get older I realize that it isn't old age that I am gaining but the wisdom to slow down, take notice, be humble(d) and enjoy the flow of life as it takes me on this journey. So Thank You to all those that have enriched my life beyond words or measure. Smile. The world may be watching!

Aug 6, 2011

A mirror can only reflect what it is shown. It does not make you fat, ugly, skinny or pretty. It does not tell you anything flattering or unflattering. It does not make fun of your rolls, bumps, bruises and cuts and scrapes. It just reflects what it is shown. What you see is the thing "Your" eyes are showing you. Take time to get to love the person you are inside and work on the one you are outside. Healthiness starts in your mind and heart. Love You!

Aug 7, 2011

Anniversary Thought: Marriage is give and take. Often it feels like you give, give, give and there is very little take from you. It is never 50/50 more like 80/20 or 60/40. It is work, it is painful and it is exhausting. You fall out of love and into love regularly. It is work. It is also the greatest thing you can have, as it is perfect, simple and rewarding. Today I say Happy Anniversary to my wife of 6 years. Thank You for being my pain.

Aug 9, 2011

A life spent defending something started with a DESIRE to defend. A lifetime journey started with a FIRST STEP. A lifelong commitment started with a CHOICE. A life of chasing your dreams first started with HOPE. Remember, to always keep your "Desire" to take that "First Step" then make a "Choice" and never lose "Hope" in your life, your loves or yourself. BELIEVE IN YOU!
Aug 10, 2011

Do not spend your life worrying about what you do not have, have not made, have not done, did not do, did not get, who you let go, didn't get to date, should have been with or things you should have changed. You may be missing the great life you have while looking for the great life you have not had. If the grass is greener on the other side it may be time to do some yard work on yours. Live Today not Yesterday!
Aug 11, 2011

A moment is a gift from time. We can squander it away, we can use it up, we can just let it be but we cannot stop it from moving on. We cannot get it back or make it return. As soon as it is gone we are on to the next one and we start again. A moment is precious and is a lifetime in itself to be cherished and used for all its worth. How will you spend your moment?

Aug 12, 2011

Faith is, believing if you are honest with yourself, your intentions and the process you are going through you will stand on the other side a better person no matter what the outcome be it positive or negative. It is knowing that through the hurt, the pain and the failures you will in fact be alright. Have TRUE Faith in yourself!

Aug 15, 2011

A hurricane can seem like a lifetime when you are in the middle of it but when it is over you can stand and recover. Life may be hard at the moment, the universe can seem to be against you but remember that no matter how dark the sky is at night the sun is only hours away. Nothing will ever hold you down as long as you KNOW you can stand up. Believe in yourself!

Aug 16, 2011

I have failed as a husband, a father and a friend. I have let down myself and those who love me most many times. I have disappointed many times and will again. However, I am not sad or upset. For every failure I have learned, every mistake I have tried to amend and every action has always been with an honest heart. It isn't the mistakes you make. It is what you do after that matters. Love You!

Aug 17, 2011

We pay attention to what's on our favorite show each week, who got booted, what celeb is doing what, we watch shows like TMZ to know everything about our favorite celebs life. However, we don't pay attention to our spouses, kids, family and friends as closely. Maybe in order to fix the world we might want to start in our own living rooms. Put down the remote, phone and magazine. Start talking to your loved ones; know more about them than the hot gossip of today. It is time for the Rebirth of Family!

Aug 19, 2011

What if there isn't a life after this? Will you have squandered away the life you have been given for one that "may" be waiting? No God has put his flock on this earth to just "make their way through" the life he/she has provided. Do not waste this life as if it is nothing more than a stepping stone to another. Respect today, and tomorrow shall handle itself.

Aug 20, 2011

There are times where we fail to say those things we wish to say. Times we hold our tongues when we should speak the loudest. Times we bow our heads when they should be held high. Basically times when we do the wrong thing. Each day I work to say the words, speak them clearly and keep my head up for you. You are the journey I take and in it I appreciate everything you do. Thank You!
Aug 20, 2011

One cannot put a cover over a broken fence and say it is fixed. You must find the root of the problem and fix that first. The same can be said of relationships of any type. If you cannot vocalize your feelings no one can help mend what has been broken. One cannot be themselves if one isn't willing to let the world know who they really are... Be Free To Be YOU
Aug 23, 2011

The moment we started to celebrate every achievement a child made is the moment we stopped raising adults who could deal with adversity. Now, adults blame everyone else for their problems and kids follow that example. A person must know how to lose, fail and recover from those in order to succeed. Life's best lessons are taught when we don't succeed. Too bad few know that these days.
Aug 24, 2011

If you spend your time searching for the world you will never actually find it no matter how hard you try or how much knowledge and materials you gain. However, if you find your true self, the REAL you, and find happiness in that person then all you have to do is open your hand and the whole world will be there spinning. One cannot possess what one does not understand. Possess You!
Aug 26, 2011

No matter how many masks you wear, how many co-signers you surround yourself with, nor how many stories you tell yourself and others, you will never be able to hide from the man/woman in the mirror. You can change it all but until you learn to look in your own eyes nothing will truly be satisfying.

Aug 29, 2011

You can open your eyes but not see, listen but not hear, be educated but have not learned. Don't try to "see" what is there, for you will miss it, take in what you hear before having something to say about it, and be smart enough to know you can learn more no matter how much you know about anything. Slow Down and Smell the Roses!

Aug 31, 2011

Do not put your faith in those who talk a good game. They can look and act strong but when you lean on them they fall or run. They can appear wise and say smart things but when you need advice they tell you what you want to hear. Surround yourself with those who are wise enough to tell you how to deal with a problem and strong enough to help you through the hard time.

Sept 1, 2011

Labor Day Thought: Be mindful that working for a goal is great but working without sight of the true blessings in your life is tragic. Take time to enjoy your spouse, laugh with your kids and catch up with old friends without the negative, the complaints or the drama but with just love and happiness. Embrace the joys of life on Labor Day.

Sept 5, 2011

Age and children are not the reason for a bad sex life in marriages. Remember the deep passionate kisses every time you kissed? The "lets run upstairs for a minute" quickies, because you couldn't get enough of each other? Remember when he was your boyfriend your girlfriends were jealous of and she was the girlfriend your boys had heard enough of? If your sex life is cold, how many logs have you put on the fire to heat it back up?
Sept 6, 2011

We only have a certain number of breaths to take in our lifetime. Do not waste them spitting hate, anger or hurtful things. Instead, use them to Love better, laugh louder and share the words that will help and heal others. The next breath isn't promised. Would you like the last one you take to be wasted? Be Better Today Than Yesterday!
Sep 8, 2011

In order to attain true wisdom one must admit they know nothing, very little or just some things but can always learn more. Never be so wise as to not hear the "message" because you have bias against the messenger. To lead you must follow. To be wise you must learn. Listen!

Sept 9, 2011

Sept 11 Thought: Service Members have been dying in terrorist attacks for decades. The Kobar Towers, the USS *Cole*, several embassy bombings, base attacks, individuals randomly killed and all the warriors who died after answering the call to go to war. On 9/11 I will remember those whose deaths have been forgotten because they weren't rich or famous but because they were doing their jobs as well as the innocent people killed on 9/11. Freedom IS NOT free!

Sep 10, 2011

As a child I was not safe to act out in public because my parents would tear my butt up. I wouldn't think of talking back, snatching away, rolling my eyes, huffing, sighing or being disrespectful because my ass would have gotten beat. There were no excuses for my behavior just ramifications. We weren't friends, buddies or hangin' partners or besties. I was "Child" and they were "Parent". Too bad so few today remember how it was to parent a child. Are you a parent?

Sept 12, 2011

Take a moment to think about all the stuff your spouse, your family and/or your friends do for you without asking for anything in return. Then ask yourself, have you been truly grateful, thankful and appreciative? Do not get into the trap of taking those little and big things people do for you for granted because you will miss it once it is gone. It is never too late to appreciate!
Sept 13, 2011

Many will say what they want to be and where they want to be in life. Many have grand schemes and plans for their future. However, one must first know where and what they are in life NOW before one can worry about the future. You cannot finish a race if you never saw the starting line.
Sept 15, 2011

We carry those we have lost within our hearts, our minds and the stories both good and bad that we tell. Though they do not walk the earth they are never truly gone from our lives. That being said, do not let the loss of someone's life stop you from living yours. The biggest tribute you can make for those who have passed is to carry on and be a better person. IN REMEMBRANCE OF THOSE I HAVE LOST!
Sept 16, 2011

Our lives are like a priceless non-rechargeable battery with only so much energy to give. Once it is used we no longer exist on this level. Spend your energy on those who would make you a better person, who love you and wish to see you succeed. Try spending time praising folks instead of bitching about folks who don't deserve your energy in the first place. Change your thinking!
Sept 20, 2011

The rarest of friends and lovers is the one who sacrifices honestly for their friends and loves. You know they are there with the truth and a helping hand when you "really" need them. Unfortunately, those are the people we take for granted most. Today, take the time to tell that person THANK YOU for always being there for you. True appreciation does wonders.
Sept 22, 2011

They say a relationship is about give and take. I think it is about giving. Give yourself to that person completely. Find out how you can make their day better and give them that. Notice the little things they hint at and give them that. If both people work to GIVE the other a better day then both people will have a fruitful and wonderful life together. Give the BEST of YOU!
Sept 23, 2011

A child does not know fear, racism, sexism, hate or manipulation. They learn that from the adults in their lives. If a parent is truthful, understanding, demanding but fair, strict but willing to listen, then a child will grow up with integrity, self-assuredness and high self-worth. Babies are born with strong minds. It is "we" that make them weak-minded adults. Time to change that?
Sept 26, 2011

Do not mistake "words" for communication. Many people talk a lot to each other but never ACTUALLY say anything at all. One cannot learn from others if one is always trying to find something to say in rebuttal of what is being said at that moment. The best of people are horrible at listening. Listening is the very FIRST step to communicating. Let us give listening a try.
Sept 27, 2011

Words are like bullets. Some can wound by the way they hurt. Miss the mark or hit an unintended target when you speak without knowledge of the facts. They can cripple/kill when they are filled with hate and venom (like from a racist/bully) and the person internalizes it with no outlet. Be sure if you point your gun you are prepared to shoot to kill, if not holster it and shut up.
Sept 28, 2011

Some people will "do" for you because they want or need something in the long run. Some will "do" for you because they have too. Then some will "do" because they really care and all they want is your happiness. The 1st will abandon you when they can, the 2nd will expect payback but the 3rd just wants your best. Make sure you nourish and cultivate the right one or you may be stuck with the wrong ones in the long run.
Sept 29, 2011

Every time someone likes my thought I personally thank them. If someone posts on my thought, I personally respond. Seventy plus Happy Birthdays I responded to each one specifically. Why? Gratitude should not be left until tomorrow it should be shared and shown daily. Someone takes time to share with you, then you should take time to be thankful. Respect starts with being grateful. Thank You!
Sept 30, 2011

Dear religious people if your mind, heart and tongue are wicked, evil, discontent, judgmental, hateful and uncaring between Monday and Saturday, then Sunday church service will not help you. No matter your religion YOUR GOD knows what is in YOUR heart and you are not fooling anyone let alone your GOD. Religion isn't a part time thing nor is it a "when God has blessed me" thing. It is Thick and Thin, Ride or Die until judgment day. What Kind of "Servant" are you?
Oct 2, 2011

When I was young we had grand and great-grandparents who we go visit and they would educate us about life in a way that 60-70-80 years of life could teach. They were our mentors and buffers to life. They are dead! Today we have grandparents who are 30-40 years old who raise their grandkids instead of being visited by them. We have lost the one thing that only time can give us from those we should love and trust: Wisdom. What a Shame!
Oct 4, 2011

For someone, tomorrow will not come. The dawn will not break on their mornings and some will not see the sunset tonight. The story of their lives will have been told with no sequels or remakes. Make sure that when it is your book that has closed you didn't leave any chapters out. Say what you wish to say, learn what you need to learn but most of all live, love, laugh and share with 100% commitment. How's your book coming?
Oct 5, 2011

A "Woman" burned her bra for equality. A "Woman" sat on a bus dog tired and help start a revolution. A "Woman" walked miles to clean houses so her kid could go to college. A "Woman" understands her body is a temple. A "Woman" raised little girls to be A WOMAN. Today, "Girls" are high on opinion and low on substance, fast to speak but slow to learn. Tops are low but self-worth even lower. Skirts/dresses are too high and lack of respect is even higher. The question is... what happened to the "WOMAN"? Maybe, it's time to teach our GIRLS how to be WOMEN again.
Oct 6, 2011

Another lost creature on this planet is the MAN. A MAN would fight if he had to but not because he wanted too. A "MAN" would work till his hands were bloody to give his family food and shelter. A "MAN" sat down his boys and told them to fight for the weak and the frail. A "MAN" knew respect for your elders, your wife and kids meant respect for him. A "MAN" had his word and it was enough. Today, we have BOYS who are BIG on Words and low on SUBSTANCE, Bulging with Muscles but lack true STRENGTH, Full of OPINION but have no real IDEA. Are PROUD to show their sons pictures but UNABLE to teach them PRIDE. Question is... If the MEN are Boys then who teaches the Boys to be MEN? WE HAVE FAILED OUR BOYS!

Oct 7, 2011

Peace of Mind can only come with being at peace in your mind. Accept the person you are but work hard to find the person you want to be. Be mindful that people can lie and be deceitful but love them for who they are anyway. Remember a journey can only end when you have completed it but, to complete it, you have to take the first step. Make today a peaceful one if only for your mind's sake.
Oct 10, 2011

We will all make mistakes in life, love and work. We will all chose the path of least resistance when the other path was the right choice. We will all go to the person who gives us what we want but not what we may actually need. We all tell stories that make ourselves look the best way possible. We are all human. Be flawed but willing to work on you. Be wrong but always work to make it right. Be strong enough to search for the truth and what you need instead of what "you" need to hear. In other words be more than human, be a Strong Person... A Leader!
Oct 12, 2011

Do not set Greatness as a goal for it is an island that only others can put you on. However, in order to BE great you must first believe you can achieve greatness. True greatness comes from a passion and desire that is deep in your soul. One can be great on small scales, be a great friend, be a great co-worker, be a great spouse or lover, be a great member of the community. In other words be a GREAT YOU today and let the others find that island for you.
Oct 14, 2011

Each day we have one absolute moment of peace when the world is as perfect as it can be during our day. It is the moment when we first wake up, that split second between dream and reality. When the day has gone the wrong way try taking the time to find that moment again. Sometimes changing how your day is going is simply changing how you look at it.
Oct 15, 2011

Military, Police Officers, Firemen/women all do something few can do. They say, "Your life means as much to me as my own and I will not leave you to die". Never underestimate the real courage of those who risk their lives for perfect strangers. Remember their spouses and kids live each day knowing they could not come home because they gave their lives for someone else. Today I salute the Firemen and women, the Law Enforcers, the Air Force, Army, Navy, Marines and Coast Guards for showing us what it means to REALLY be AMERICAN. Thank You!
Oct 17, 2011

Make not an issue of something and it can never be an issue at all. Make it an issue once and it will never be a non-issue again. Not everything that happens in your life deserves your complete energy, half-energy or, in some cases, any of your energy. Put things in their proper place and deal with them accordingly. Though it is fun, one does not need a shotgun to kill a fly.
Oct 18, 2011

Ever fear the truth? Ever wish you hadn't learned something about someone you trusted or loved that destroyed you? People fear the truth but there is not a reason to do so because it does not hurt. The truth can sting the eyes and ears and even pierce the soul, but the pain you feel is never real because the "truth", like love, never really hurts. Be brave enough to demand that those around you speak the truth to you, and you will find that the "truth", can in fact, "set you free".
Oct 19, 2011

People are pissed that schools are teaching about "homosexuality". When my parents were kids they could not learn about BLACK history because it wasn't "AMERICAN" history. Sadly, we are no more tolerant to those who are different than we were when the KKK walked freely in the streets and attacked blacks. One cannot ignore what exists but one can sit down, discuss and be educated on things they do not understand. Fear and condemnation of the unknown is more rampant today than ever before as we continue to move backwards as a society. Shame!
Oct 20, 2011

Ladies stop complaining about all the worthless men out there in the world. No one made you pick that man nor did they make you have a child with that man. If you continue to complain about how crappy men are in your life maybe it's time for you to change your criteria for what is "good man". A good MAN isn't worried about his pants sagging he is concerned with his children learning respect and education. He isn't worried about impressing the homies he is worried about making you better than before. He works with you to build a strong family. HOWEVER, take the blinders off ladies because a lot of you don't know how to TREAT a good man when you get one. Remember, it isn't always the man that is causing the problem. Perspective Matters!
Oct 21, 2011

MEN! It is not <u>MAN</u>ly to get a bunch of girls that you do not love nor plan to spend your life with pregnant. It is not being a MAN because you buy your son (and sometimes your daughters) the newest clothing or the nicest jewelry. It doesn't take a man to teach a child to fight but it does take a man to teach a child to fight for those who cannot. A MAN may have to take the backseat for his child's sake but a man will never disappear on his child. MEN teach Honor, Loyalty, and Respect for themselves, their women and children. Above all else A REAL MAN displays those things. Will the REAL MEN please STAND UP!

Oct 24, 2011

Many of us ENABLE people especially loved ones under the title "love". To enable is to handicap the person through our own weakness to do what is right. When we don't make our children take care of their responsibilities such as taking care of their own kids, we cripple our kids. When Grandparents spend more time with grandkids while mom and dad are hanging out, we cripple our kids. When we give them money even though we know they blew their paycheck on lottery tickets and smokes, we cripple our kids. In short, when we FAIL to make our children deal with THEIR consequences for THEIR actions, we cripple our kids. It takes strength to do the right thing; it takes weakness to enable. ARE YOU STRONG ENOUGH? Oct 25, 2011

A common problem with us today is that we "Expect" too much for ourselves and "understand" too little about others. The world revolves around ALL people not just one person. That "stupid waitress" you just left a penny with could have a mother dying in the hospital. We never know other's pain or problems as they don't know ours. Today, try being a better HUMAN and think more about how you are to others rather than how they are to you. A frown or bad comment goes far but a smile and well wish goes farther. What kind of HUMAN will you be today?
Oct 28, 2011

Halloween Thought: Remember when you weren't too old to dress up? When you didn't feel uneasy about walking around looking silly? When your entire week was set on a 2-3 hour walk with one big pillowcase? Remember back when you and your friends mapped out the neighborhood for the good houses to go to? It is Halloween! Pull off the tie, take down the hair and be a child for a little while. Happy Halloween my friends. May it be frightful and delightful. BOO!
Oct 31, 2011

One should never give what they cannot afford to lose be it your time, your money or your heart. If you are there for someone consider it a gift without strings. Do not expect the same in return if the roles were reversed. Expectations of equality can end long-standing friendships and relationships. Instead of getting upset understand that not everyone you have been there for can be depended on when you need them. In short, Be aware of the walls (people) you can lean on when you are not strong enough to stand.
Nov 1, 2011

When I was a child I hated my father for spanking me and lecturing me at the same time. Today, I understand ownership of my actions. I hated going to my grandparents for boring long lectures. Today, I know true respect for my elders. I hated the neighbors who told every time I did something wrong. Today, I understand it took a village to raise THIS man. In school I hated friends who were two-faced and talked behind my back. Today, I know how to stand on my own beliefs and not bow to peer pressure. I hated when the coach wouldn't let me play even though I thought I was better than the others. Today, I know you don't always get what you believe you deserve but you always get what you work for in the long run. I learned because I was guided, taught and shaped and now I TEACH. What are you teaching?

Nov 2, 2011

When you have died and the story of your life is being told will you be proud of the journey you took or ashamed? Would you have spoken with truth and integrity or have kept silent and lied? Will you be proud to sit front row and take a bow at your premier? Each day we have a chance to be more than we were the day before. Today, take the time to write a journey that you can be proud of when it's over. As I say, Be Better Today Than Yesterday!

Nov 3, 2011

How does one justify being part of a riot? How does Freedom of Speech over rule one's Freedom of safety? When did we get so lost in bitching and complaining that we forgot how to effectively make change? It doesn't matter if you are the 99%, the 1% or the .001% if you resort to crapping on the rights of your FELLOW American then you are no better than those you oppose. Maybe we should try being part of the 100% American where we make change for the better of all of us and not just ourselves. I am Sean and I am part of the 100% American! Nov 4, 2011

Love with 100% of your heart. Love through doubts, through pain and through deception. Listen intently, understand completely and forgive honestly. Then expect the same in return. Remember, people are flawed and make mistakes. Be willing to forgive and forget. If all else fails, Love YOURSELF enough to walk away. In short, Love the way you truly wish to be Loved. Enjoy what you have because tomorrow it could be gone. ONE LOVE!
Nov 5, 2011

If your marriage is unhealthy, your kids our out of control, your relationships with friends and family are merely tolerable or of convenience, you are struggling to make ends meet and living check to check, you have little or no communication in your home, your home is in disarray, you job is in shambles and your outlook on life is generally grim this is for you. Stop worrying about Kim Kardashian's failed marriage, Lindsey Lohan's arrest, the housewives of whatever, what others should and shouldn't be doing and FIX YOUR OWN STUFF! Today the saying of "Get some Biz of your own" has never rang more true. To fix the world we must fix ourselves first. Am I talking to you?
Nov 7, 2011

The problem in many families, relationships and associations is that we do not know how to express ourselves effectively. When someone hurts your feelings do you lash out? Do you get an attitude? Talk bad about them to others? Take it out on those who are weaker than you? Post it on FB? Majority of conflicts are due to miscommunication and lack of understanding. Never speak when angry because your only goal would be to hurt. Never react without thought on why you were hurt. Try to understand the other person's point of view before making your case. Lastly, be open to being WRONG and be strong enough to APOLOGIZE if you were. A lot of bad in relationships of all kinds can be fixed if we stopped to THINK before we acted. Just a thought!
Nov 8, 2011

Veteran's Day Thought: The greatest gift an Airman, Marine, Sailor and Soldier ever gave was "Freedom". The 99% may never know what it is to not eat for days, carry a wounded friend out of a fire fight, and stay up with him till medical arrives only to have him die before it does. They will never understand that a kid gave her leg, her arm and possibly her life so they can complain about free healthcare. We are a FREE country because of the Brave men, women and families of our US ARMED FORCES. Freedom has never been and never will be FREE. To all my former, present and future services of this great nation's Armed Forces... HAPPY VETERANS DAY on 11/11/11.
Nov 9, 2011

Thanksgiving Day Thought:

Someone lost their spouse tonight which they will never see again;

Someone lost their child tonight to a cancer fight they couldn't win;

Someone bought a ring for his love but never got to get down on one knee;

Someone will never walk again after an accident took away that ability;

Some young girl will never have a magical first time because someone stole it today;

Somewhere there is an entire family starving in the worst way;

Somewhere there is a family laying down to pray for a parent fighting a war;

Only to find that that prayer will be unanswered as two uniformed men knock on the door;

Somewhere a woman will have given birth to a baby whose heart will never beat;

Somewhere the most caring grandmother in the world would pass in her sleep;

So as you sit with your families, friends and loved ones on this night;

Take a moment to be truthfully Thankful for the blessings in your life;

Remember that tomorrow isn't promised to any of us and this moment could be our last;

Be Thankful for the greatest gift of laughter and love you got and all the joys of your past;

And Today I am THANKFUL for my wife, my sons, my family and my dear friends;

Grateful you have all made me a better person if we never see each other again;

To all those who read my words I am grateful to you too;

Because my words would have little meaning to the world if it wasn't for all of you:

HAPPY THANKSGIVING MY FAMILY AND FRIENDS... Most of all the MEN and WOMEN of the ARMED FORCES of the USA.

Nov 25, 2011

Remember when you kept your personal business in the house? Your kids knew that you didn't tell folks about what went on in the house. A husband spoke to his wife and a wife spoke to her husband. Posting how you done with men or women on Facebook only makes you look foolish and desperate. Maybe it is time to stop proclaiming love, giving yourself over and praising these men and women before you know them in the first place. Keep your business in your house and the world won't be all up in it. It is time for grown-ups to start acting grown.
December 6, 2011

Many people complain about "Christmas." They say "Christ" has been taken out of it. These are the same people who got into shouting matches on Black Friday. The same people who have 200 gifts under their tree though they are struggling to make ends meet. Same people whose teenage daughters have "no tan-lines" and sons show of their butt cracks. Same people who condemn people for talking trash only to talk trash about people. So again this is for my religious folks... Before you put CHRIST back into Christmas try putting him back into your homes. For everyone else, Christmas is about giving to those who don't have, sharing love with one another and celebrating the human spirit of understanding and hope. It is not who can buy the most stuff or who can offend whose religious belief better. Merry Christmas, Happy Holidays and all the other ways we say it.
Dec 7, 2011

Your life should be like the sands of the beach. Strong enough to hold, soft enough to allow you to leave your mark but wise enough to erase your steps as you continue moving forward in life. Remember yesterday's lessons, pay attention to today's teachings and never underestimate the power of teaching tomorrow's courses. BE AMAZINGLY YOU!
Dec 13, 2011

When will people realize that the person who speaks out against something the loudest and most passionate usually is the last person you should follow? Before you stand by someone because they appear to be on your side first know WHY they are on your side. No matter how you spin it, making a deal with the devil is never as good as it seems and will often leave you screwed in the end. Make a stand for those who cannot, speak for those without voice and live for those who are no longer with us. However, KNOW who you are following before they lead you off a cliff! Just a Thought!
Dec 15, 2011

A REAL Friend's Promise: I will always say what I believe you need to hear not what you wish to hear. I will be honest with you even if it cost our friendship. I will strive to make you the best person you can be. I will not co-sign everything you say because I know that we can all be stupid at times. I will not support your destruction be it drugs, alcohol or any other similar thing. What you tell me in confidence will stay there but I will tell you if that secret is wrong. In all I promise to be a real friend and hope you can give me the same. A REAL friend wants you to be better not to just feel better. What Kind Of Friend Have You REALLY Been?
Dec 19, 2011

A Parent's Promise: I promise to raise you to be able to stand on your own. To teach you how to be strong, compassionate and independent not weak and greedy. I will not live my life through yours and I will not make you my best friend. I will allow you to fail and allow you to stand back up because that's how you learn to succeed. I will give you advice for the rest of your life that is best for you and not me. I will not support you being a drug addict, a criminal or any other useless person in society. I will stand by you at all times with all the love I have. I will expect you to treat your spouse, friends, family, elders and people with the respect and compassion I taught you at all times. I promise not to let you live in my home as an adult nor will I raise my grandchildren as if they were mine because that is their parents' job. Most importantly, I will teach you to respect yourself at all times. In all, I promise to Love you enough to not need me when you leave the nest but be strong enough to know I am there when you really need me. This is MY promise to you with Love.

Dec 20, 2011

A Mate's Promise: I promise to never take for granted the small things you do on a daily basis. I promise to never stop dating you. I will ask you what you want and always give you what you need. I will never say to a friend or anyone else something about you or us that I do not intend to talk about with you. I promise to be honest with my feelings, express my pain and heal our wounds. I promise to forgive when I say I will, forget when the time is right and remember relationships take work. I will remind you that you may not be perfect but your imperfections are what I love. I will fall in love with you over again every day. I will never put anyone above you be it friend or family. Most importantly I will walk in front of you when you need me to lead, behind you when you wish me to follow and besides you at all other times. In short, I promise to make you the Queen/King that I always said you were. This is my "Mates" promise.
Dec 23, 2011

Thoughts go out to my wife's cousin whose 12-year-old daughter was diagnosed with a very aggressive form of Cancer. Her vibrant life and goals have all been changed a couple of days before Christmas. So I ask that if you pray that you pray for this young girl to have the strength and determination to fight through the pain that is to come. As well as for her family who will have to endure the agony of seeing an innocent child suffer and fight. If you do not pray then please give a moment of thought to the young lady. Remember tomorrow is not promised to any of us so make today worth what we pay for it. A heartfelt love and appreciation to all of you. Merry Christmas Eve! Dec 24, 2011

Merry Christmas to all my friends all around the globe;
Merry Christmas to those friends of friends and those I
don't know;
Happy Holidays to you, May you find the peace and
happiness you deserve;
With joyous smiles of those who love you and those you
wish to serve;
May your spouses and mates smiles light your day as they
open gifts;
And your children's laughter and squeals of joy keep you
in Holiday bliss;
Here's to never being too old to get a gift from good ole
Saint Nick;
And being young enough to get on the floor and play with
silly gifts;
Most of all Merry Christmas to those who have traveled
on to the Pearly Gates;
The one's we will see again but now live in the memories
that no one can take;
Merry Christmas to those who are fighting wars and will
not see the gifts opened today;
But will eat with fellow Airmen, Soldiers, Sailors and
Marines and make it special anyway;
So one last time from Sean, Keziah, Sean Jr. and Trae;
Merry Christmas to one and all on another magical
Christmas day:
December 25, 2011

Trust, like Love, is given freely and completely at first, strengthened by actions, hard to break but easily destroyed and takes a lifetime to rebuild. So, when someone gives you a genuine chance to make amends for doing them wrong do not ruin it by being dishonest, deceitful, evasive, not owning up to your actions or doing what you did to lose their trust. Losing someone who believes in you is a void you can never refill. Cherish that friend, family member and/or spouse who believes in you enough to work through trust issues because when they are gone you will never fill that void. Trust Me On That!
Dec 28, 2011

Final 2011 Thought: Take the time to remember all the choices you made this year that were mistakes. Recall the moments that made you cry or made you sad. Think of the times when you worked hard but didn't get what you thought you should have gotten. Remember all your failures. Now erase them! Hold on to those moments of 2011 that turned out perfect. The moments that you laughed until you cried and made you happier than ever. Think of all the times when someone said Thank You for something you did this past year. Remember all your successes. Each year you have the opportunity to grow, make a difference and be better than you were before. My final thought of 2011 is remember the good in you, the great in others and the joys of living and then take that from 2011 as you wave goodbye to it. 2011, YOU WERE AMAZING! (Thank You all for reading my thoughts this year. I appreciate it)
Dec 31, 2011

2012 Thought: New Year's resolutions are fool's gold. Do not promise to lose a bunch of weight or be a better spouse, parent or friend. Don't say you are going to call people or stop cursing. None of these things last. Instead, Be honest with yourself. Listen to those who take time to talk to you. Surround yourself with those who will help you grow not those who will keep you where you are. Find balance in your life and try new things. In short, make today better than yesterday for everyday this year. Grow internally as a person, as a husband/wife, as a parent, as a boss/worker, and as a friend. Be more than you thought you could be but not more than you should be!

Jan 4, 2012

TAKE STOCK! How much energy do you give to negative and hateful people, events and things? Do not waste the energy of the day on things that do not make you smile, laugh and feel loved (Blessed for my religious folks). If you allow the negatives of the world, the day and the situation to take your "happy" then you have failed yourself. Remember Love conquers all while Hate eats away all it touches especially the one who spreads it. What will you spread?

Jan 9, 2012

If I told you that you only had 1 million tears to use before you would die would you continue to waste them on those unworthy of them? If I said your life force would end on a specific day would you spend your energy on people who don't make your life meaningful? If you were only given time to speak to 10 people before you passed would you waste it on hating someone, telling someone off or would you spend it spreading love and wisdom? The most important question: Should you have to be asked these questions to do what's right? It's Time to Live Better!
Jan 11, 2012

If someone, especially a mate, says you are not like someone else it is less about what you are and more about what they are not. Do not allow yourself to be what "someone else isn't" in a person's life. Always demand to stand on your own merit in any relationship be it personal or professional because in the end you are better than a stand-in.
Jan 13, 2012

Martin Luther King's dream died when we started standing for the wrong things. We have race riots because a drug dealer and gangbanger got roughed up by a white cop. Yet, we don't stand up to the gangbangers and drug dealers poisoning our neighborhoods. We write long thought out complaints over celebrity gossip but fail to write a single word in support of teachers in our schools. We yell at the government (which we should) about resources for our lower classes but don't support programs to get youths off the streets and into classrooms. Dr. King wanted us to all be equal but to be equal we need to RAISE our standards not expect others to LOWER theirs. All of us be it Black, White, Indian, Spanish, Mexican, Italian, German, Asian and all races in-between need a reality check on what it is to be "People". I have a dream that one day we will stop making excuses for our failures and start making progress with our hard work. Rest In Peace, Dr. King!
Jan 17, 2012

Relationships are like a flower garden. You have to pay attention to it, take care of it daily, replenish it when needed and clip the dying pieces to keep it fresh. If you are lazy, it will become overgrown, sloppy and weeds (other men, women and interests) will consume it until it is no longer recognizable. Then the only thing left is to get a new garden. Your husband/wife are your roses that need constant attention to grow full, beautiful and life lasting. If your garden looks like crap maybe you should stop crapping all over it and do some work! Just a thought!

Jan 21, 2012

A stay at home mom of 10 years loses her spouse. A man working at a company for 15 years is let go. Cancer hits a parent and medical bills are piling up. Wife loses a limb in a warzone. All these things would change your way of living in the blink of an eye. Many don't know what to do when the world "all of a sudden" changes for the worse. In life you need a plan B, a backup plan, a new approach and a way to "rebound". No matter how many times people say "I am there for you" the fact is they won't be for long (if they are smart). You need to have a marketable skill set or have a needed college degree to fall back on but whatever it is "have a plan". Isn't it time for people to start depending on their own ABILITIES instead of hoping family, friends and/or the government will "help" them out?
Jan 26, 2012

Ever think about the promises your man/woman you have on the side makes to you? Many people "creep" and they believe all the glitter that "other" person sells them. However, if you got into a car accident and your face was forever burned would they still tell you that you are beautiful? If you got testicular cancer and could no longer make the bed rock would she still love your touch? If you were bedridden from spine disease would they wash you after you had an accident? We give people credit for promises they "never" have to keep because you belong to someone else. Before you throw away what you have, ask yourself one question. If tomorrow came and I was the opposite of what I am today, who stands by me when I need them most? Remember the last thing you want to find out when you are down and out is that you chose the wrong team to make you better. Those who love you love you through it all. Which LOVE are you holding on to, the real one or the fake one?
Jan 30, 2012

What are you "really" teaching your kids? We say stealing is wrong! Why do you have a house full of stolen movies and music? We say respect others! Then we walk by people and can't even speak. We say get good grades in school! When was the last time you sat and read with your child, helped them with their homework or even really knew what they struggle in? The question is how many of you live by the motto "Do as I say not as I do"? Kids today lack respect both in self and others, discipline, integrity and self worth all masked behind a bunch of talk and no real action or substance. Think it's time for the parents to start to "Teach" them by EXAMPLE. Just a thought!

Feb 2, 2012

A lot of people are concerned about the mixing of their personal and professional worlds in mediums like Facebook and Twitter (etc.). The issue should not be that "your boss saw your inappropriate comment" but more that you felt the need to post something inappropriate that you "cannot" stand behind. Never say or do anything from the privacy of your home on a public forum that you couldn't say or do in public. Private means "private" and not for "friends of friends" as we have on Facebook or "Retweeting" like we have on Twitter. The fault lies squarely on your shoulders if you chose to hit "post" and hoped it would only be between you and your 325 friends. Just a thought!

Feb 7, 2012

(Relationship Week) When was the last time you made the day about your spouse? I'm not talking about the occasional flowers or card or "here honey we can have sex". I am talking about giving her/him a bath, a massage, their favorite dinner, sending the kids away for a day (or half a day) so that you can spend time alone in the house. As Valentine's Day approaches think about all those things you have taken for granted from your spouse. Things like meals, laundry, household repairs, getting up in the middle of the night for each other and even the "I Love You's". Take the time today to think of how you can once again make your spouse feel "special" and make it about them not because it's Valentine's Day but because they "deserve" it. Live Freely, Laugh Always and Love Authentically! Just a thought!
Feb 13, 2012

Valentine's Day Thought: So many have lost the point of Valentine's Day. It isn't about the flowers or the candy for bragging rights to the girls in the office. It isn't about the expensive dinner in the overcrowded restaurant where you can't enjoy one another's conversation. It is about the moments where you find the little twinkle in her eye you loved so much or the boyish grin hidden behind all of his "tough" exterior. Valentine's Day is for those who love each other, to enjoy one another, like it was a new relationship again. It isn't about the kids or competition amongst friends. When this Valentine's Day comes to an end ask yourself these two questions. One, did you GIVE or do something that was truly special and relit the flames of your love with your mate? Two, did you RECEIVE or get to do something that was truly special that relit your flame with your mate? Maybe more marriages and relationships would continue with the fire they started with if instead of following commercialism of a holiday they followed LOVE(ism) of one another. Do something out of the ordinary for your Love today. Happy Valentine's Day Friends!
Feb 14, 2012

V-Day Thought for my Wife:

A wife can make mistakes and make everything a little better;

She can bring a smile to your face with words that are funny and clever;

She is the mother of our children and the keeper of our hearts;

She is the best of thing to happen to man, where do we start;

Her smile brings a smile and her laughter makes you laugh;

She can bring you from your darkest places even when you are mad;

She will take on the world and often won't say a thing;

She will hold your hand to make you feel better even when she is in pain;

Many buy flowers and cards, candy and jewelry to show they care;

But Today I will forgo all that and just say I am blessed we are a pair;

So Happy Valentine's Day dear wife, your value can never be replaced;

I can find no greater gift in the world than putting a smile on your face:

-Your Husband!

Feb 14, 2012

(Relationship Week continues): Time to reflect! Ladies, now that Valentine's Day is over and you posted all your proud pictures of what "your mate" has done for you I want to ask a question or two. Was the day about how people viewed your mate and in turn how they viewed you? Did your mate buy you something unique that was from their heart or did they "have to" buy you a certain thing i.e. flowers and candy? How many put in the same effort for him that he is required to put in for you on this day? Was it about rekindling the love you two share or was it about the commercialization of another "for her" holiday? Today, take a step back and see if yesterday was about the "two" of you (or 10 of you if you are in Utah) instead of the public perception. A relationship is about the love of two people and Valentine's Day should be a rekindling of the real flames of being in one another's company and embracing one another to feel the "one heartbeat". What was that backbone of your day? To all those who loved authentically I say congratulations on putting another log on the fire. Be mindful my friends of the purpose of your needs and desires. Just a thought!
Feb 15, 2012

If one took away your money, job, car, house, make-up, jewelry, and any other thing that defines you, what would you be? Breast implants and liposuction, big muscles and big money, platinum watches and expensive diamond rings, expensive cars and awesome toys all are great to have earned but are also great to hide the person inside. A man/woman should not be defined by the things they have but by the thing they ARE. Do not allow your "image" to take away from the one thing that makes you amazingly special, yourself. Maybe it is time to start being REAL individuals instead of real good at copying the status quo. Just a thought!
Feb 21, 2012

When did it become OK to stop believing in the possibilities of life? We all have dreams of being something be it a movie star, a doctor, a writer or a world traveler. Think about how many things you have pushed over your dreams, how many excuses you have made to keep you from achieving them and how many times you have had the chance to take a step towards achieving them. Today, take a moment to dust off that old imagination and find some of those hopes and dreams you let die and bring them back to life. Life is short, and tomorrow is not promised, so make the most of it and take that amazing leap! Dream Big, Friends!

Feb 23, 2012

We are a generation lost. Men and Women use to grow up to "have" something in life. A better life than their parents and grandparents had before them. Now, we make excuses for our lack of success. We want handouts instead of working for what we want and need. We placate our children with electronics at every turn instead of talking to them. We mooch off our parents be it with money (we never pay back), living with them or having our kids live with them. We are no longer "people of our word" but people "full" of words. It is time for my generation to stop crying about what they don't have, stop babying these kids and stop driving these grandparents into the ground with "our" problems. Let us stop trying to redefine what a "Man/Woman" is and should be and start actually being real Men and Women. Just a thought!

Feb 27, 2012

Respect is the one thing you cannot take, you cannot demand, you cannot force it. It cannot be bought no matter how much and it cannot be sold or passed on like an heirloom. Respect has to be EARNED by your words and your following actions. Today people believe respect is given because "everyone deserves it" but the truth is fewer and fewer people deserve it in today's world. Today's thought is a challenge to those of my generation and younger. Sit down with a person 60 or older and ask them what "respect" means. Then take that knowledge and "share" with the world. RESPECT should be the last word we let die in our lifetime. Maybe it's time to resurrect its true meaning and teach these kids.... Just a thought!
March 6, 2012

There is a big difference between someone accepting who you are and someone lowering their standards/opinions to accept who you have become. When a loved one stops doing the small things, stops needing to hear the special words from you and stops being upset when you have done something wrong then they have lowered their expectations of you. The worst thing someone can take back that they gave to you freely, after Love, is pride. Remember we cannot always help who we love but we chose those who make us proud. How do people look at you?
March 19, 2012

The Trayvon Martin case has reminded me of one undeniable thing. We are all blind sheep. I grew up with friends shot and killed in gang violence. I saw young girls prostituted on the streets and beat up by pimps and johns. I watched police canvass the neighborhood for clues only to have no one speak up. Yet, when it is a black vs. white thing the nation is in an uproar. The media and those with a hidden agenda are playing us like fools and we are simply smiling and saying, "Thank You". I don't know if Trayvon was a menace, a gangbanger or a threat. all I know is a man killed him and that needs to be properly investigated. I don't know if the man is a racist, a bigot or even a tax evader. all I know is he chose the role of neighborhood "protector" and in that he has repercussions like any of us that are sworn to protect. He chose to shoot like he was a police officer and thus he must be accountable like one if it was unjustified.

All that being said, I want to know how many of the people "reposting" this divisive issue has also been speaking out against the filth in their own neighborhoods? How many would lie and protect a relative who committed murder of an innocent person? How many times have we looked the other way when it was a black on black, white on white, Hispanic on Hispanic or similar crime? Am I the only one that finds it remarkably sad that the only time we get in an uproar is when we can place a "Racism" tag on it? How many Muslims and Arabs have been beat and killed in this country since 9/11? Where is the uproar?

This thought is not against finding justice for Trayvon Martin because any unjustified killing is wrong. This thought is to point out the "sheep" mentality so many of us live with and spread. When is it going to be time to stand up and just fight for what is right because it is "right"? I don't know what is sadder the fact that another child was killed or the fact that people are going to turn this into another Race Riot? Just a thought!
March 26, 2012

When one decides to look the other way on what is right and just in the name of justice for a wrong doing they have proven without a doubt that they are no better than those they have protested.

Back to the Trayvon Martin case, my fear of ignorance spreading like wildfire to the sheep that have followed this case in the bias media's form of laying crumbs out for ants have been founded. I find it hard to believe that people just shake their head in agreement to the Black Panther Party putting a hit on Zimmerman. I find it shocking that few have called Spike Lee out for posting on Twitter the address he believed was Zimmerman's because he was "angry". When is ok to say no justice no peace? So many people have turned injustice into Justified Ignorance and Hate. Would we stand by and support the KKK putting a bounty on a Black man accused of killing a white kid like being reported about the Black Panthers? Would we stand and support a media that reports stories for their fantastical nature rather than its accuracy of reporting? Once the word is out it is out it can never be changed and the minds of the ignorant will continue to go unchallenged. How many of us have sat in our living rooms or our cars and spouted our racist views about cases like this without ever considering the impact on your kids, teens and young adults? Many adults would swear on a bible that they would never put a loaded gun into their children's hands because they or someone else might get hurt. When we spread the disease of hate we are loading our children themselves with bullets that can only hurt them and others. Why would we load our kids with some much more dangerous than any gun?

People need to understand that gaining a victory while giving up your moral and ethical ground is not gaining a victory at all. What happens if some young teenager decides that $10k would be great for his family and kills Zimmerman? Would the same people who are screaming so loud wish to have those who set this act in motion punished too or will we turn our eyes and say "he had it coming"? What happens if then if the KKK puts out a hit on an accused Black, Hispanic or even Asian male for killing a "innocent white person"? Do we turn the other cheek and say "eye for an eye"? The point of today's thought is to say demand justice for those who have been done wrong but do not lose your principles, morals and sense of humanity in pursuit of it. The slope we walk as a people (that means all races) is a dangerous one when we start justifying evil to combat evil. Just A Thought my friends!

April 9, 2012

A Love that has never been questioned, never been doubted and never been threatened with loss is a love that has never been tested or proven. Love isn't about how you live in the sunshine and beautiful days. It is about how you stand in the dark and stormy weather. What kind of Love do you have?
April 20, 2012

Relationships are like your gardens as your spouse and children are their very own flowers. Each flower needs special attention and care. Our children need constant support to grow strong enough to stand on their own. Our spouses need constant attention to ensure weeds (outside influences) don't begin to take over. A beautiful garden takes time, patience, a great deal of attention and work and not one thing can be more important than the others. How does your garden look?
April 25, 2012

Few people truly have people in their corner that love them enough to stand next to them through all their tough times and can forgive them for taking them for granted. However, sooner or later even the most caring and understanding people get tired of being kicked in the face. You will have no greater loss than the loss of someone who believed in you. Take care of your treasures, my friends. So who are you taking for granted?
May 8, 2012

Mother's Day Thought: Wanda Brown gave birth to me and guided me to the man I am today. Edwina Brown became my step-mom and helped raise me. Kathy Woodside became my mother-in-law and kept me under her wing. Sheryl Woodside gave birth to Keziah Brown, my wife, and now looks down on us from heaven. Each woman, strong in her own ways, was devoted to teaching me how to stand on my own two feet and to stand by my word. Each passing a torch of how to treat a woman and how to make her worth more than anything else I could possibly want in life. Each my Mother! So, Happy Mother's Day to Wanda, Edwina, Kathy, Sheryl and my wife Keziah.   My life's journey would be empty if it weren't for the strong women that have led me along the way. Thank You for being wonderful Moms whom I hope are honored to have me as a Son (and Husband for Keziah). To everyone else, Happy Mother's Day to all those who deserve it!

May 13, 2012

One will never be able to see the Truth "of the" Matter when all they ever see is the Truth "as it" matters! If we spend our lives being right that means everyone else is wrong and thus we are never able to see, hear or understand the truth of the matter. How many steps do you need to take backwards to see the big picture? Remember communication starts with listening first and speaking second. Just a Thought My Friends!

May 15, 2012

Memorial Weekend Thought: I stand at attention and salute all those who have gotten up and put on a uniform with honor and integrity. I say Thank You to all the mothers, fathers, sisters and brothers who have had to say goodbye to a loved one who paid the ultimate sacrifice for our freedom. I shed a single tear as "Taps" plays as I stand in front of another display of a pair of boots, a rifle, dog tags and a helmet for another fallen comrade. I whisper, I am proud to have known you to MSgt Steve Auckman (5th ASOS, Iraq 2004) and SPC Dennis Poulin (181 Infantry Afghanistan 2011) for showing me that freedom has a heavy price tag. This Memorial Weekend I ask that you all to personally Thank men and women you see in uniform for their service today, and then Shake the hands of any Veteran you see both young and old because without them there would be no United States of America! May we never have to bury another Airmen, Sailor, Marine or Soldier from combat but if we do may we NEVER FORGET what they gave. Just a Thought!

May 28, 2012

We have lost the "teachers" for this generation. I remember back in my teenage years my pants would sag, I would act like I knew it all and be big, bad and tough around my friends (and enemies). However, my actions did not go unchecked and I wasn't free to "express myself" at will like so many kids today. My parents and even adult neighbors would scold me and my friends for talking like an idiot saying things like "dis, dem and A'ight" like so many of my favorite rappers would say in their songs and interviews. My father, uncles and grandfathers would say stuff like, "when you become a man you will understand how to dress and how to act like a real MAN". Their pants weren't hanging off their butts, they wore shirts with collars, and suits with dress pants and ties. It did not matter if you were Black, White, Mexican, Asian or any other race and it didn't matter if you were a CEO, a mechanic, a teacher or a janitor at a school they would hold themselves as MEN. They would tell me, as I get older I would understand that a man with his own home, his own car, a job that meant something and a family to take care of and raise needed to set THE example. He

should teach his daughters how to cherish their bodies and his sons how to respect the women they chose in life as if they were his mother or grandmother in both respect and pride. He taught integrity and ownership in his kid's actions and he preached the value of being better than those who sought excuses for their failures. Today, men who are 30, 40 and even 50 years old dress and act like the teenage boys of when I was younger. They stand with little to zero integrity, intelligence, pride or ownership for anything that is deeper than superficial "bling" that we see from celebrities and athletes. If we don't find MEN who covet things deeper than a flashy car, the quick money or banging everything that moves, be it female or male, we are destined, as a species, to crumble. Want proof? Look at the kids out around your own town and look at the sad excuses we call parents these days. Something Has Got To Change! Just a thought!
June 8, 2012

Father's Day Thought: In life you can be a leader of people from your job to your community but the most important leadership position a man can have is that of a Father. As a Father you protect, educate, discipline, hold, mold and love. You are the riding horse, the evil spaceman, the giant and even the jungle gym. You can be scary when mad but the biggest kid in the room as well. Our sons grow up to be like us and our daughters grow up to marry a man like us. We are "Dad", "Pops" and "Old Man" to those little look-a-likes that we helped bring into the world. So to all the real leaders of the land, Happy Father's Day!
June 17, 2012

Advice is like a bullet. It is safest when kept inside. Once it is given it cannot be taken back and you must live with whatever it strikes both intended and unintended. Be mindful of where you point your "Advice" because you never know what collateral damage you may cause when you fire it off. Just a Thought!
June 19, 2012

If men are the lost "teachers" of this generation then the woman is the lost "soul" of this generation. The WOMAN has always been the soul to our society. It was her will and determination that kept the family together. It was her touch that made even the toughest man calm down and it was her word that taught us compassion, humility and understanding. She was not defined by her cleavage nor how short her skirt could be to show off her "assets". She did not have to stand in front of the world and tell everyone what a great mother/wife she was because you saw it in the actions of her children and spouse. She was not her kids "best friend." She was their Mom. She stood for everything that was right and would not tolerate anything less from her children. She knew that even though she was a mother she was also a spouse and she took equal care of both her children and her husband/mate. In return they took care of her. She is a dying breed! Today we have cougars and such trying to be like teenage girls with everything they have to offer on display. Our school age daughters look more like strippers than women. They are violent and lack any form of real self-respect. Today's girl rather leave her child(ren) with her parents while she "enjoys" life. She talks about being a great mother yet doesn't have the respect from her children or her mate. Today my thoughts are on the matriarch of the family because she is sorely missed. If we don't start teaching our young girls how to be actual women I believe there will be no hope for us as a people. Let's bring our SOUL back. Just a Thought!

June 27, 2012

July 4th Thought: The American flag flies from my home every day of the year (except in the rain), it is illuminated each night and it is replaced when it has become too worn. My flag represents the men, women and families both in uniform and civilian service to the armed forces of this nation and their sacrifices they have made for our freedoms. Today, I say Thank You to all that have defended the freedoms we cherish (and abuse) most. Happy 4th of July to my friends, family, and fellow military members fighting the fight all over the world and those not at war. Raise a glass for those who have paid the ultimate sacrifice. POW/MIA gone but not forgotten.
July 4, 2012

Strength cannot be given, it cannot be sold, it can not be bought or passed down. It can only be earned through hard work, determination, blood, sweat and tears. Each difficult moment in your life has made you stronger and in that you will gain true strength to carry on. Life may drop you to your knees but as long as you stay strong it will never put you on your ass. Be strong my friends!
July 11,2012

We shall never be a people of freedom if we cannot be a people of mutual respect and admiration. In competition we battle wits, strength, commitment, allegiance and overall skill with representatives from countries across the globe. We march in one country after another in a line of unity, respect and brotherhood to battle for Gold, Silver and Bronze but more importantly Pride of country. Today, I wish luck to all the men and women who have made it to represent their countries but the greatest luck to those who adorn the colors of Red, White, and Blue. May all of our athletes represent what it once meant to be an American and what it means to be prideful to represent our flag. Opening ceremonies start today, GO TEAM USA!
July 27,2012

We should all strive to approach life like a baby. A baby is not born with the ability to walk so it must sit there and observe the world as it is without being able to change it. A baby is not born with that ability to talk instead it must listen intently to the sounds of the world in order to find its voice. The baby does not know prejudice, hate, discrimination or lies these are things it will learn as it observes the world. Maybe it is time we forget how to speak, stop running away and just sit and see the world as it is today. Only then can we start to hear, understand and comprehend the changes we need in not only others but ourselves. Just A Thought!
August 21, 2012

Today will be one of those days where people show humility, they will share stories of sadness and pain with strangers and friends alike. Today, the news will show that clear blue New York sky forever painted with the evil dark black smoke that would turn to grey and brown clouds of debris and dirt flying from buildings collapsing. Today, many of you will post pictures of Firefighters and Police Officers who said, "I can save one more" and risked everything to do so for perfect strangers because it was simply, their job. Today, many of us will refuel that anger we had at the cowards who killed so many innocent people in an attack on not the American people but the American Ideals. That, my friends, is the problem! Today, many people will recharge their anger instead of finding their love for one another. On September 11, 2001 the USA saw the diverse people of a great nation come together and say, "We will not let you hurt our brothers and sisters again". As a people who are Black, White, Hispanic, Asian, Native American, African, European and all races in-between. We stood as Catholics, Baptist, Buddhist, Christians, Jewish, Non-believers, Satanist, Scientologist, Zealots and yes, even Muslims to show that in America we all have the right to live free and peacefully. On that day, we were truly "AMERICAN". So today my friends I am asking that we remember 9/11, we remember all the men and women who have given their lives in defense of our beliefs, our freedoms and our American way but most of all remember the split second the country put aside their prejudices, their hate, their me-first attitudes and just reached out to help their fellow countryman.

Thank You to all those who have sacrificed the ultimate sacrifice like the men and women of the Armed Forces, the first responding police officers, firefighters and medical personnel, civilians who have given just as much and especially the families of all of them who knows that each day word could come that another sacrifice has been made for our country. Thank You to them all. Never Forget 9/11!
Sept 11, 2012

Yesterday, someone thanked me for my sacrifice for serving my country and after a moment I thought this: I did not sacrifice to serve my country. Instead I chose to stand in front of a nation and say, "I got you!" I did not ask to give my life. Instead I chose to say, "your life is just as important to me as my own." I did not put on a uniform, shine my boots, cut my hair and make sure everything was in perfect order. Instead I said to those before me, "I wear this with pride, honor and respect because of you who wore it first." Then, after my thought I calmly said to the person, "You are welcome!" I did so because not everyone has what it takes to be an honorable Military man or woman or as the Marines say, "The Few and The Proud." So Thank You to those who sacrifice to serve this great nation. One Brotherhood, One Sisterhood- Air Force, Army, Navy, Marines, Coast Guard! Oct 21, 2012

A Veteran isn't a person who simply puts on a uniform. No, a Veteran is someone who put on a uniform and served it with integrity, pride, respect and poise. A Veteran leads by example and follows with absolute certainty that he or she will get the job done. A Veteran worked long hours, missed important family events, sacrificed a great deal for the simple act of "Doing what was right". A Veteran didn't always agree with the Leadership or the Supervisors appointed over them but they always supported the mission and made sure their Brothers and Sisters in Arms were safe. A Veteran wears a "Retired" hat every day of his or her life because once you served honorably you forever serve. A veteran is humbled when someone says, "Thank You for your Service" and usually answers something like, "I didn't do anything it was team." A Veteran gets up in the wee hours of the morning to get the job done even though their body is aching from years of service, injuries affecting them long after they retired from service, and memories of horrible nights still vivid and fresh in their minds. They get up and work. They give every ounce of their being to do things for themselves, their families and others. A Veteran is a Veteran 24 hours a day, 7 days a week, 365 days a year and even after the death they still represent the Armed Forces of the United States of America. A Veteran isn't just a uniform it is the Men and Women whose heart beats stronger, faster and more sincere for those who say, "Please help us we have lost hope." Happy Veterans Day my Brothers and Sisters in the Air Force, Army, Navy and Marine Corps! It is because of YOU that I stand proud a Military Veteran! And a special Thanks to the Husband, Wives and Families of the Veterans who have served: You are the silent Military Force that each of us live and die for. Without you all we would have nothing worth fighting for. Thank You Too!

November 11, 2012

Thanksgiving Thought:

I am Thankful for all the blessings that I have in my life;

My sons Sean Jr. and Trae and my amazing wife;

I'm Thankful for my military friends spread across the globe;

Who helped me to grow from a young fool to the man you all know;

The military family from Lakenheath and the 48th Fighter Wing in the UK;

To the 51st Supply Squadron at Osan, Korea and Chem Warfare ladies from back in the day;

And the 5th Air Support at Ft Lewis with my brotherhood of TACP's;

Along with the 1st and 3rd Brigade soldiers of the US Army;

Then my Expeditionary Port Unit 114 from Sub Base Pt. Loma in San Diego;

That welcomed me in the brotherhood of the Navy and taught me all I know;

Also, my newest Brothers from the 1/81 Infantry Yankee Division out of Boston, Mass;

Who will forever have my respect especially SPC Dennis Poulin who died on that mountain pass;

I am Thankful for every Airman, Sailor, Soldier and Marine who stand with dignity and pride;

That continue to defend freedom at all cost, May you all stay safe during your military ride;

Most importantly I want to Thank my Family and Friends for standing next to me;

You are the true meaning of Thanksgiving because of all the love you allow me to see;

Happy Thanksgiving to each of you who pass my page may you remember what it is really about;

Not the things we have to show the world but the things we can't live without;

So may your Turkey be juicy, your stuffing be tasty and your yams sweet as a first kiss;

And your crazy uncle, aunt or grandma stays out of the "sauce" and get pissed:

Happy Turkey Day Fam.

Nov 21, 2012

Six months ago I stood in the white structure over the USS *Arizona* at Pearl Harbor. As I stood in my own silence looking at the rusted ship below me I could feel the pain, the loss, the sacrifice and the heroism of that day, Dec 7, 1941. As I looked at the wall of names that remained in the bowels of the ship below me a thought came to me, "May I never have to give as they have for my country, but if I have to. May my sacrifice forever be remembered as I defended my nation I love so dearly." I sat on that monument for 30 minutes without saying a word. I didn't hear the people around me nor did they even exist. What I heard was the men and women (2404) who died on that day. I was honored to stand with them even for a brief moment to say Thank You. Today, I look to the heavens to salute those who gave to make the Red of our Flag a little brighter. Your sacrifice is not forgotten.
Dec 7, 2012

I do not pray nor follow any particular religion, however, I ask that God (from all denominations) to look over the families of the people killed and hurt in Connecticut today. A child is innocent from racism, hate, prejudice and evil. Today, the world lost more innocence as one man decided to leave a mark that will forever stain many lives. May whichever God you pray to give you the answer to why we as people have failed one another so greatly. Maybe it is time to stop thinking about "me" and start thinking about "we" as God intended. Just a thought!
Dec 14, 2012

I want to wish a Merry Christmas, first and foremost, to all the Men and Women who are serving in the US Military all over the world. Thank You for your continued sacrifice for all of us. Secondly, Merry Christmas to all the Police officers, Firefighters, Nurses, Doctors and all the first responders who spend their holidays working long hours away from family and friends to keep us safe. We often overlook all of these who sacrifice without complaint, with little pay and not enough appreciation. Take a moment to say a prayer (if you pray), share a thought (if you don't pray) and say Thanks (if you see one) to any of these great people who sacrifice to protect people they don't know. Lastly, I want to say Merry Christmas to my Wife, Sons, our parents, family and friends. May we all strive to be better people, better citizens, better friends and most of all better neighbors to each other. Thank You all for making our year wonderful. May 2013 be even better.

Dec 24, 2012

New Year's Thought: 2012 has seen the worst of humanity. We have had major natural disasters, war, murder, rape, debt, greed, destruction, hate and downright evil spread across the globe. The wicked have spoken with both religious and nonreligious tongues. Our televisions have broadcasted the "evil that men do" 24 hours a day and in High-Definition too. And we, as the people with the voices, have mutilated the good, perverted the innocent and condemned the well meaning all in attempts to justify our own beliefs and existence. Yes, 2012 has been a year among years for the self-centered, egotistical, illogical, immoral and plain sick men and women of our species. With all that 2012 also so the greatest forms of humanity after natural disasters. It saw the unity of brother- and sister-hood in the eyes of destruction and it saw Love. 2012 was a year of that will not be again and it is time to put it to bed. Here is to hoping that we all take time in 2013 to be nicer, live kinder and search for wisdom to help one another. Make 2013 about spreading laughter for good reasons, love for love's sake and joy because we wish the world to be joyous. Take time to learn about those you do not understand instead of condemning homosexuals as degenerates, Muslims as the enemy, Christians/Catholics as close minded hypocrites and many, many more like it. May you all find the strength in 2013 to ask "Can I help you?" instead of "what can you do for me?"

To all the Men, Women and Families of the Armed Forces I say may 2013 find you all safe, sound and eventually home when you need it most. For all those who have died in 2012 fighting for something other than themselves I say a heartfelt, "Thank You for Your Service!" To all the one's I have served with from the Air Force to the Navy to the Army and even the Marines I say, "May you all continue to inspire the world as you inspired me to continue to serve this great nation." Lastly, to all my family and friends I say, "Happy New Year, May the path to your success be full of lessons that make you better, stronger and wiser. May we all grow for 2013!" Happy New Year people....Just a thought!
Dec 31, 2012

Nothing holds us back as a society more than our uninformed opinions of others. Instead of casting a stone of judgment to those you do not know or understand try casting a hand of introduction. The only way we move forward is through mutual respect and understanding. Just a thought my friends.
Jan 15, 2013

MLK Thought: "I Have a Dream" was echoed through the Lincoln Memorial on that August day in 1963. Many believed that with the election of President Obama that MLK's dream had been actualized in this great nation. Many believe that today we have found equality with the people of the United States of America. Unfortunately, those "many" are wrong because MLK's dream has not been realized it has been bastardized, misrepresented, misunderstood and just plain missed. We are no closer to equality today than we were when Hitler was putting Jews in ovens, when Native Americans were being slaughtered like animals for land, when Blacks were being hung and beat for crimes not committed, when the Asians were forbidden to come to this country, when the Mexicans were forced off the lands they too had claimed for the better of a nation, when women were nothing more than keepers of the home but voiceless in the public and the many, many more held back people of the past including many whites. Yes, MLK spoke of freedom of the slaves but it was more than that it was for the freedom of all of us. Not the freedom of "doing what I want to do" but the freedom of being able to "do what I need to do for the better of us all." The freedom to pray to God, Allah, Jehovah or no one at all if that was the preferred choice. The freedom of respect for each other as "one" people no matter the skin color, the background, the race, the religion or the sexual preferences of any one. Yes, Blacks have been freed but the prison of the mind in the neighborhoods has been just as deadly as any whip from a slave master. Yes, Native Americans have been given land but the lack of education and over abundance of drugs and alcohol has been just as deadly as the "Trail of Tears" so many years ago. Yes, Whites have open their doors and hearts to their fellow people but the shame of slavery has stunted the harmonic growth of all the people of the nation as we all hold on deeply to the past while never looking at the future. Yes, Chinese and Japanese have been able to find their place here but American greed has now made them, Chinese especially, the enemy of a nation indebted to them. MLK's dream died when we became a nation of finger pointers instead of a nation of helping hands. Look at the comments on anything posted on web and you will see hate, vile, anger, impatience and insensitivity, lack of respect or dignity and just plain ugliness. This is America. This is the "Freedom" that has been founded in the deep roots of our own fragility. Today is Martin Luther King's day and in that I give praise and respect to the man and the many people who followed to try and make equality a real thing. I Have a Dream that one day we will stop pointing fingers at each other and start listening and helping one another. MLK's "Dream" can still be had but it takes people, all people, to put aside their stupidity, judgment and hate for the better of our "species" as a whole. I HAVE A DREAM my friends... Just a Thought!

Jan 21, 2013 MLK Day

Yesterday I woke up at 0445 and put on my Navy uniform and headed into duty. I would head to the Reserve center, cram into a crowded desk and begin my exam for E-7. This happens every year (since I never make E7) but yesterday was different. Yesterday was February 10, 2013 and it happened to be the 20th anniversary of the day I left home and joined the U.S. Air Force. In that time I have made friends I call brothers and sisters. I have said farewell to many but two in particular, MSgt Auckman (5th Air Support Squadron) and SPC Poulin (181 Infantry Y/D). I have been molded into the Sailor I am today because of the great Air Force, Army and Navy leaders and subordinates I have served with over the 20 years. I have been told I have helped make other's careers something to be proud of and for that I am Thankful. Most importantly, I have had the privilege of serving with honor and having a career I can be proud to call mine. I still have months (maybe a year) left before I finally call it a career and walk away but today, one day after my 20th, I want to say Thanks. Thank You to all the men and women who I have served with from the 48th FW, 51st Supply Squadron, 5th ASOS (1st ASOG), EPU-114, PRT Kunar and all the many, many places I have been in-between. Lastly, as any military member who has served can tell you a very special Thanks has to go to my wife (Keziah), kids (Lil Sean and Trae), my parents (all of them) and friends who wanted me to be more than another Los Angeles statistic. So if you have served with me or supported me and are reading this with all the humility I can muster I say, "Thank You!" Just a thought my friends. Feb 10, 2013

It does not matter to me if you are for or against gay people being able to marry. It is your "right" to be for, against or neutral for your own reasons. However, for those who are standing on top of their religious teachings using it as "the" reason for being against I have one simple reminder for you. God does not differentiate between "SINS." So while it may be an abomination to lay with a man as one would lay with a woman, in the eyes of God, it is equally as wrong to not live as he commanded. In short, do not condemn to hell those who may very well be your roommates in the afterlife. How's your glass house today? It's just a thought my friends.

March 29, 2013

Easter Thought: The story of the resurrection of Jesus is also a life lesson for us all whether you believe in a God or not. We are all capable of letting the person we are today die and becoming the person we always dreamed we could be. On this Easter Sunday take a moment to give Thanks for your God, Thanks for your family/friends and a special Thanks to the person you are striving to be. May you all be resurrected into better husbands, wives, mothers, fathers, brothers, sisters and friends. Much Love to all of you. Happy Easter. Lastly, on April 1, 2011, I got confirmation of the passing of SPC Dennis Poulin from the 181st Infantry serving in Kunar Province in Afghanistan. A special Happy Easter to the families of the men and women who have gave their lives so we could be safe. Thank You Brothers and Sisters of the Armed Forces.
March 31, 2013

Mother's Day Thought: You will never see my mothers talk about what great moms they are on Facebook. You won't see them post pictures or re-submit quotes talking about how hard it is being a mom. They won't stand up and make a scene when it is their kids time shine. You won't hear any excuses for my actions that I made of my own choice. They will not take care of my children when I am capable of doing it myself. They will give me advice as a parent but never try and take over what is my job. They will correct me being rude, disrespectful or out of line. They will never ask to be celebrated for what they did to make me who I am because who I am is what they celebrate. Today I say Thank You to the Women who helped me grow . And because of them I want to thank a special mother, my wife, for carrying on the tradition of strength with our boys. My good woman does not walk behind me she stands right next to me as we stroll through life. Thank You to the very special MOTHERS in my life.

May 11, 2013

Memorial Day Thought: The beginning of June 2011 I finished my RR and returned to Afghanistan. On the C17 along with 130+ other military members were two aircraft pallets containing nearly 20 military coffins each. On the way back these coffins are stacked 5 high and strapped on like another piece of equipment. However, the next time one goes on a plane it will have had been transported in a stripped down Hummer, carried by 8 military members, slowly marched through two rows of 40 plus military members onto the back of the C17 aircraft. Once on the plane the Chaplin, First Sergeant and others speak solemnly about the "contents" of the container. On top of the cold silver container is a crisp brand new American Flag. Outside the plane stand rows and rows of both military and civilian personnel paying their respects. The "contents", as I noted, is a man or woman who had paid the ultimate sacrifice in a country far away from home.

My return trip to Afghanistan was accompanied by 40+ temporary homes of fallen members of the Army, Air Force, Navy and Marines. Memorial Day is about these heroes and the millions who have died before them for this nation. As I stand as 20+ year Veteran I snap my boots together, raise my right hand to my brow, salute and give a heartfelt Thank You to all those who have served this great nation. Most importantly to the men and women who have given the ultimate sacrifice and the families who carry their memory. We should never need a "day" to celebrate those who defend and fight for the freedoms that many of us take for granted. As you enjoy your BBQ's and cold beverages take a moment to say Thanks! Just a thought my friends!
May 24, 2013

Memorial Day Thought Too: A friend of mine posted a thought remembering those who have fallen defending this nation. In response a friend of his "thanked" him for his service in which he replied "I didn't pay the ultimate sacrifice! I simply partook." I sat with that for awhile and realized something very important. Memorial Day is about the men and women who took their last breath on the battlefield, the oceans deep or the blue skies over the land. It is about those whose bodies were never found and those whose bodies made the long solemn journey home under a flag draped coffin. Yes, Memorial Day is about the legacy of the United States Military member who wrote the check and paid up when the "balance was due." Memorial Day is also for those who didn't pay the ultimate sacrifice but sacrificed nonetheless. It is for every military member that has woken up in the middle of the night because they thought rounds were coming in. For every one who jumps into a defensive posture when something scares them. It is for those who held a comrade as he/she lay in blood wishing he/she could just "go home" knowing he/she is about to die. It is for those who come back home and never make it back to "normal" life. It is for those who could no longer take it and tragically take their own lives to end the noise, the hurt, the pain, the dreams and the fear. No, my friend was wrong he didn't simply "partake" he, like millions of others, sacrificed a lot for our freedoms. So this Memorial Day I say Thank You to all those who paid the ultimate price and all those who stood up and said they would too. Be Safe, Be Smart but most of all Be Appreciative of what that flag really means to those who serve it. Just a thought my friends.
May 27, 2013

Father's Day Thought: Men: A Father is a man who will teach his son how to stand for something worth standing for, defend something worth defending and love (completely) someone worth loving. He will teach him to respect first his mother(s), grandmother(s) and sister(s) so that he will know how to treat and respect his wife (or husband if that is his preference) when he has the honor of having one. He will teach his son to speak with honor, pride and to carry the family name with dignity so it can be passed on with pride. A Father is a man who will teach his daughter how to be strong when no one else has strength, how to believe when all faith seems lost and how to love and be loved in the way she deserves. He will teach her that her body is a temple not to be displayed for the world to see but to be respected for those worthy of it. He will teach her the type of man she deserves to have instead of the type of man she has to settle for. He shows her how a man should love and respect her by the way he loves and respects her mother because he is a MAN. Not everyone can be a father! Don't say AMEN yet!

Many fathers are not allowed to be in their children's lives because of petty Bullshit between the mother and father.

This Father's Day my thought is for all the parents who spend more time degrading the man (and woman) that they share a child with instead of speaking kindly or holding their tongue. Every time we speak ill of the Father or Mother of our children in front of, around or directly to our children we are diminishing the child's self-worth. Remember a child is the COMBINATION of their parent's not just one. So when women call their babies daddy a worthless piece of shit remember the child(ren) are also being called that too. When a man calls the mother of his child(ren) a stupid whore and bitch then he is also saying about his children. This Father's Day let us take time to thank the men who teach the boys how to be men and the girls what a real man is through their actions and not just their words. Happy Father's Day to all the men who try their damndest to be a part of their children's lives at all cost. This Father's Day take the time to check how well we are all doing as parents. Just a thought my friends!
June 14, 2013

I saw this woman with this low cut shirt showing just enough cleavage to make this old man look twice. Her tiny shorts showed off shapely legs and just a little glimpse of her shapely butt. Her makeup accentuated her eyes and pouty lips. Even her hair was formed in a way to show off her sexy and sultry side. If I wasn't married I would have taken her home. Of course that is if I wanted to not only piss off my wife but to spend 20 years in jail for statutory rape. Why? This sultry, sexy and amazing woman was thousands of young girls walking around our streets today. Young girls from all ages are pranced around in makeup, sexy clothes, low- fitting tops showing off their cleavage, extra short skirts they can't bend over in or skin tight pants that in days of old would get "yeast infection" warnings from older women. Shall we teach our young women what once seemed to be commonplace many years ago? That the more they physically show to the world the less the world sees them for who they are as a person. Maybe we should stop trying to be MILF's, GILF's, Cougars, Lions, Tigers and Bears (oh my) and start once again teaching these girls actual self-respect. It's just a thought my friends.

June 25, 2013

4th of July Thought: May those who have fallen be forever remembered by those who had to carry on. May those who carry on be forever cherished by those they protect. May those who are protected forever honor the freedoms they have been presented. May we all take the time to remember that being American isn't about race, religion or anything else so trivial. It is about those who stood up for those who couldn't. It is about helping one another to be better people, neighbors, friends and citizens. Today take a moment to Thank the Men and Women who serve In the Armed Forces and those 1st responders who risk their lives as well. I personally want to Thank MSgt Steve Auckman (5th ASOS) and SPC Dennis Poulin (PRT Kunar/ 181 Infantry) for their ultimate sacrifice. You will always walk with me. Happy 4th of July my friends.

July 4, 2013

I'm perplexed. Do people really want "Justice for Trayvon" or do they really just want to promote "racism" at all cost? Why aren't we seeking "JUSTICE" for the hundreds of kids murdered by gang and domestic violence every year in every neighborhood of every city in the US? My 16 year old nephew had, from what I recall, 3 friends die by gun violence last school year but there wasn't any community outrage to catch the killers. So many of these murders go unsolved because people don't want to get "involved" or be "snitches" when it comes to talking to the police. Then there is the Martin case where George Zimmerman ignored police request and continued following the young man which eventually ended in Martin being killed. Yes, Zimmerman overstepped his neighborhood watch role and should be punished for it. He wanted to act like a cop he needs to be held accountable like one. That isn't in question. The issue, for me at least, is that had Zimmerman killed a white kid he (Zimmerman) would be considered Hispanic. He killed a black youth and now he is white. We have once again fallen into a trap of complexity where simplicity would do perfectly fine. Make both of these guys the same race and the story would have been nothing but a footnote. No matter what happens in this case the seed has already been replanted. If Zimmerman doesn't go to jail for 50 years to life then it is the racism of AmeriKKKa (saw it spelled like that on a friend's page) coming to the front again. If he does go to jail then it is "finally" a white guy goes to jail. No matter the verdict, in a week we will have moved on to something else. So my question… Do we really want justice for Trayvon because it is the right thing to do or do we just want to continue curling up on our couch with the warm blanket of racism? And for clarification racism is definitely alive in many of our minds. The sadness of the death of a young man can never be overlooked. So yes, we need "Justice" for Trayvon but remember that when the gunman is of the same race in your city and you have the power to do something about it. Right is Right and Wrong is Wrong my friends.

July 12, 2013

Yesterday I turned 39 years old and it got me reflecting on the changes in our society over that time. When I was a child and teen I had to have not only respect for my parents but for ALL adults or people of authority. I did not use words like what, huh, nah, shut up or whatever to my parents or siblings (in front of my parents that is). If I ran around stores, shops or restaurants I would get my butt spanked (sometimes in the bathroom of said place). Even today, I have to show my parents, grandparents, aunts and uncles the same respect as if I was still a young boy. Knowing your place is important in life. As my 38th year rolled to a conclusion I see that level of respect is dying. It is choking by the very words and attitudes we allow to spill and spew from the mouths of children, teenagers, young and old adults. The freedom to do what we want, when we want and how we want seems to be the voice that speaks loudest. As my 39th year begins I can no longer sit back and simply watch the murder of something so important to me, respect. Respect must be resuscitated and given its life back at all cost. We must give the voices of right, leadership, man- and womanhood, ownership of actions and community uplifting reprieve from the unjust prison they have been locked into under the guise of "That's how they use to do it." So I have decided that in my 39th year I will do what has been given to me as a talent/gift that I only use so often. It is time to finally write my book in a hopes to share the wisdom (or opinion at least) that I have gained over my years. My birthday gift to me is to finally stop waiting for the right time while passively posting "thoughts" about what we, as a people, are doing wrong. It is time my friends for me to do something important to me. Thank you to all my family and friends for the great birthday wishes. I appreciate it. Lets see what the next 365 have in store for me.

Aug 7, 2013

(Side note: Book is being written Feb-May 2017.)

Early this am I was awaken by a jolt and an explosion (bang). My first thought when I woke up was to grab my M4 or 9mm. I began to survey my surroundings realizing that I was not in a wooden cave of a room but my spacious bedroom. Once that realization set in I did the house check (still not knowing what the hell happened). I went outside to see if the explosion had gotten my neighbors out. There was no one outside. At this point I am wondering if I dreamt it all. Finally Trae came down and asked if I "felt that." Apparently, we had a little earthquake (3.9 last report) and the "explosion" was Trae's globe falling off his bookshelf. All this took less than five minutes but the reality of it did not escape me. Everyday men and women of the armed forces struggle with the idea that they are no longer at war. They reach for their gun, they jump from loud noises and they dream of explosions, sirens and overall chaos of war. So today's thought is for those who know, spend time with and/or love members of the armed forces who have seen combat. No matter how long it has been since they have returned the scars of war remain like a wound that will not heal. The inner struggles of those that sacrifice should never be overlooked, understated nor forgotten. It takes love, patience and understanding to help those fighting the internal battle. Not everyone can laugh off the thought of "grabbing his/her gun" like I did this morning. PTSD has many levels and stages and every member needs support to continue that fight to deal with the scars of war. To all my military friends: You are not alone. Just a rambling thought my friends. Now time for coffee.
Aug 22, 2013

There's a couple of things I have some thoughts on, that I was going to start with, like the "issue" with the beating of the WWII Vet in Washington State (coming to you Trayvon/Zimmerman folks). However, my FB has been blowing up because of the VMA performance by Miley Cyrus. People are in an uproar over her performance calling her a slut and showing the awesome Smith families (Will, Jada and the kids) reactions. I've heard people call her parents horrible and useless because they allow their daughter to act such a way. Oh the stones that are cast are many, forceful and downright vicious. But then I thought what about the mirror? You know the mirror we all stand in front of as we let our own underage children were shorts that their butt cheeks hang from under, low cut tops and skirts, and skimpy bikinis on tanning bed tanned bodies. Do these same people stand on their pulpits of righteousness when it is their own kids, friends' kids, or kids' friends who are dressed like "sluts"? I am baffled how easily people can stand so high when others are involved yet are meek as a mouse in their own circles.

How many of these people have no idea what pictures their kids are sharing on Instagram, Facebook and text? Are these the same people who let their children listen to Chris Brown who, mind you, went Iron Mike Tyson on his on-again and off-again girlfriend? What about the housewives of (pick a damn state) or any of the reality shows? I guess it is that Hannah Montana is a role model most parents can't be for their own children. Miley owes these mothers an apology for not teaching their daughters how to be women. Anyone think Will Smith's daughter is available for teaching our daughters? How about Selena Gomez? Moms are too busy passing judgment and casting stones while being MILF's and just plain "hot" to be parents. Damn, Miley, you should've known better. Off I go to see all those moderately dressed girls at my son's middle school. Good thing morality is still alive! Rant over... For Now...

Aug 26, 2013

As I sat and watched TV Montel Williams came on to tell me how me being in debt is "not my fault." Then I saw a loan consolidation commercial which also told me that it isn't mismanagement of funds that has me in financial hurt it is just life getting to us good people. In short, "it is not my fault." Then I saw a commercial with a young boy who was having a hard time keeping up in school because, "the teachers couldn't teach me the best way." Or (yes, you guessed it) "it is not his fault." The more and more I watch tv, listen to the radio, read online stories the more and more I see someone telling me that "it is not my fault."

It dawned on me that we have all fallen into a mental trap of acceptability for mediocrity. If a child does not succeed in class, more often than not it is not the teacher's fault. Maybe parents should spend more time helping kids learn than buying them stuff. If a husband and wife are having issues it isn't the "others" fault. It is on both of them. There are so many things I can use as examples but the truth is we need a mirror because it IS OUR FAULT. We are responsible for kids that get bored and beat a WWII

veteran to death. It is our fault that our children and young adults have little to no respect, not only for others, but themselves. It is our fault that grandparents don't have money because they are RAISING their grandkids. It is our faults that these "boys" are grown and living in mama/grandmama's house while making all these damn bastard children that they refuse to take care of. It is our fault that these young women talk about self-respect but have absolutely no clue what it truly is or how to demand it. It is time to stop making excuses for our failures as guiders of the future of our society. It is time to start walking the walk. Don't worry if you can't though because I am sure "it is not your fault." Just a thought my friends.
Sept 2, 2013

Sept 11 Thought: Here we are with another day for people to change their profile pics, share some Meme of burning buildings and overwhelming support for our men and women in uniform. This is it! This is what we have become when a catchy slogan "Never Forget" is the most important part of remembering. 12 years ago we were attacked by cowards who hid behind the Muslim faith and attacked innocent non-combatants. The planes plummeted out of the sky and the buildings crumbled to the ground. At that moment Americans united for a common cause of taking care of "all" of our people. We flew flags because being American meant sacrificing for the greater good of THIS country. It doesn't mean forget your Irish, Asian, African, Indian, Mexican etc. etc. etc. roots in any way. It means know where you come from but realize where you are AT because you are an American.

Sadly today we are no closer to coming together than those buildings were to staying up after the planes hit them. We will never be able to stand together if we are too busy condemning each other over our beliefs. Have we forgotten that America is a melting pot of all the great parts of the world brought together in one place? A Christian and Muslim should be able to sit down and have lunch without condemnation of each other's practice in faith. The men and women of the Armed Forces protect EVERYONE'S rights. We do not put our lives in harms way to back one group or one power. In fact we fight for those who cannot.

So, today on this September 11th, I ask you all this: What are you doing to make our world better? For all those that died in the attacks I say, "Rest In Peace." For all those who have died in fighting the wars after I say, "Thank You for your sacrifice." Lastly for all those who use this tragedy and our military men and women as some sort of launching pad for your personal agenda I say, "Fuck You!" May we all learn how to live with each other in understanding rather in judgment and condemnation. Just a thought my friends!
Sept 11, 2013

There are things we do in life that we can be "passive" with and other we have to be "active" with in order to make them work. We can be passive with FB (I'm always on), Twitter (heck no), Instagram (really no), Candy Crush (Ok, level 492), fantasy sports (nope again) and similar things. If you could not do any of those things your life would not end though so may think so. Two things we cannot be passive with are PARENTING and RELATIONSHIPS. Right now I want to hit parenting. As parents we have gotten into a system of placating our children with electronics and, even worse, leaving that responsibility to others like teachers or neighbors to teach them their values and morals. The more we allow our kids to slip into the depths of disconnection within the connected virtual world the less they are prepared for real life. We need to take parents back to the time where they (the parents) are in charge and the values, morals, respect, responsibility and ownership are passed down from them to the child(ren). We have taken away our own powers and passed them to the virtual world of idiots and fools in the hopes that those very fools will teach our children better than we can. Our children are not our friends nor business partners that we negotiate with they are the heirs to our legacy that need to be taught humanity, humility and honor. Children with respect and internal strength are almost as rare as Bigfoot sightings or Mars moon landings. So the question is my friends, what have you given your children? Have you given your children strength, compassion and understanding of values and morals that will carry them into adulthood or have you given them the excuses to fail? What say you friends? It's just my thought.
Nov 6, 2013

Veteran's Day Thought: I am not a Hero. I do not wear a cape nor have super powers. On Feb 10, 1993 I was a young, arrogant, cocky kid who decided to join the US. Air Force. At the time I was just trying to escape the streets of Los Angeles so I did not become another jail or cemetery statistic. The transition was hard for me, in fact, one of my first supervisors threatened to kick me out every other day. Thankfully, there were many people who stepped up and guided me to be more than that cocky kid. After many years I became something more than my city, my hood and my upbringing. I became a defender of our Freedom.

Early on I did not appreciate that honor but now I know what it is to be a defender of Freedom. I am not a hero. I am a defender and a protector for those who cannot or will not sacrifice for the freedoms many of us take for granted. I am part of a team of Airmen, Marines, Soldiers and Sailors who stand tall and say, "Not on my watch." These are my brothers and sisters who are nothing more than men and women who want to see the children of tomorrow have the freedoms of today for another day. I am not a Hero. I am just a simple kid who grew up and said, "I swear to defend..." No, I am not a Hero. I am much more than that........... I am a VETERAN!

To all the Veterans past, present and future I say, "Thank You!" May we all be wise enough to understand that it takes a special breed of person to add the RED to our flag. We are Veterans and this is the weekend we get to say Thanks to all that put on a uniform of this United States of America. Thank You! (We should all rock a vet picture for the weekend. If you aren't a vet then rock one you know or just a flag to show support for those who serve/served.)
Nov 8, 2013

How many of your insecurities do you make your spouse (sig other) be responsible for? I'll have more on this but I am curious where this question may/may not lead... What say you friends?
Nov 15, 2013

You cannot truly love someone else if you do not love yourself. Too many people put their happiness in the hands of significant others, children and/or friends yet fail to put it in their own hands. Love created by others can be taken by others. Love created within can be taken by no one no matter what that person meant to you. If you want to repair your relationships on all levels, the first place to start is within........ Who do you love? Just a thought friends.
Nov 20, 2013

Up to this point we have had the pleasure of having one holiday that could not be perverted by the mass exploitation of people's gullibility by big/small business. Year after year for one week we, as people, would find the basic lessons our grandparents-grandparents taught from so many years ago. We took the time to remember those who have left us and those who are with us still. It is the time to share laughter and good food in a moment of fellowship and brother/sisterhood. It was a time to get past the stupidity of trying to one-up each other and just to love each other.

Over the past few years stores have pushed their "GET THE BEST DEAL" sales to the day after. Now, that has moved more forward as the one day that could not be sold or made-for-profit is becoming less and less

important. Thanksgiving is two days away yet by the commercials and FB updates of pre-pre-pre-pre-pre Black Friday sales one would think Christmas is two days away. Christmas lights, presents and music run rampant in all stores and even in homes. Thanksgiving is dead. There are people camping out in front of best buys and stores of the such in order to get their Black Friday (which is now on Thursday in some places) deals. We have sold our souls to the "deal" and in it we have killed the values that were once one of the most important lessons of life, gratitude of the things we cannot buy not even with 100% discount. I'll have a Thanksgiving Day thought soon but today I just want to share a moment of silence for what seems to be a holiday that is slowly having the life stolen from it. How do we get back to the things that build our character, our family bonds, our friendship and our overall humanity? Just a thought my friends
Nov 26, 2013

Thanksgiving Day Thought: Happy Thanksgiving my family and friends and friends of friends. Today, may we all remember that today is not about the "deals" we can get at those super sales by all those stores that care about us oh so deeply. It is not about the football games, the basketball games, the hockey matches or even the big juicy bird that cooked for so many hours. It is not about remembering what the white man eventually did to the Native Americans. So many of us have tried to make it about one, some, all or a myriad of similar reasons to celebrate but those reasons come up short of the truth.

Thanksgiving is about the humanity that we as people, not as a race, share with each other. It is the time to take a day and remember that a hand extended to teach a foreign people evolved to the melting pot that we have today. Thanksgiving is to celebrate the family and friends that bring the joy in our lives, the pep in our steps and words written in the chapters of our lives. Thanksgiving is for humility and homage to those that have passed on the wisdom of decades lived to be carried on by those with decades left to go. It is Thanksgiving.

Today, I am Thankful to my wife and sons for making my life a fun ride of laughter, love and silliness (mainly caused by me :) I am thankful to all those who taught me how to be a man, a husband, a friend, an Airman, A Navy man and even a Soldier. I am thankful to all who join my "Sean's Thoughts" and choose to have adult discussion on whatever my brain brings up. Most of all I am thankful to all those who bring light to my day in ways that provide the fuel to every ounce of my being. Happy Thanksgiving my family and friends may your turkey be moist, your dressing be great your teams win (as long as they aren't playing mine) and may your family and friends all feel the love you have for them. Also, Happy Thanksgiving to the family of my fellow sailor who will spend Thanksgiving praying for him to wake from his coma and smile once again. Lastly, Thank You to all those first responders, military, nurses, doctors, police officers and such who spend the holiday working to keep us all safe. You are an underappreciated few. Thank You! Have a good one friends! Thank You all!
Nov 27, 2013

If you haven't smiled authentically, laughed wholeheartedly and shared a joyful moment with someone then you have already wasted too much of the day in the wrong way. Go out and make someone smile, laugh and see what happens in return. The difference in a great day and a bad day is often in the way you approach the day!
Dec 02, 2013

When having a bowl of cereal one must be careful to not run out of milk because one does not simply add more milk. However, if one runs out of cereal before running out of milk then......ADD MORE CEREAL.... That's all. Now more peanut butter crunch is needed.
Dec 11, 2013

So with all the controversy of the comments made by the Duck Dynasty dad I thought I would chime in. Initially I wanted to talk about the people screaming "First Amendment "as if Freedom of anything absolves a person of responsibility of what they have said. I was going to jump all over that but instead I really have to make a point to the war on "Christ"mas. The hypocrisy of people is amplified on this particular holiday more than any other. People are pissed because someone says Happy Holidays or uses the term "Holiday Tree" because they are taking Christ out of the holiday. So I ask, when did Christmas become a holiday to overspend, to have the best lights, to prove who has the best elf on the shelf but more importantly to celebrate consumerism instead of the actual Birth of Christ? Having "Christ" in Christmas means to have compassion for others even if they believe something other than you do. It is to say Happy Hanukkah to someone because you know they are Jewish. It is saying Happy Kwanza because you know the person celebrates Kwanza. It is saying Happy Holidays because you know the person simply celebrates the season of giving. It is respecting that others are wishing you and yours well no matter what you celebrate. If you believe there is a war on Christ then maybe it is because so many "believers" have forgotten what it is to be God-like. As Christmas approaches let us remember that we are suppose to help those who are without what they need. We are to share the joy of life (and God if you are a follower) to everyone. In short we are suppose to prove that we can actually love each other as was intended for humanity. Maybe we should spend less time worrying about a rich group of duck guys and more time worrying about the degradation of our humanity towards each other. Happy Consumerism Day Friends!

Dec 22, 2013

Merry Christmas to all my friends and family. I hope that this day reminds us of the simple pleasures of a child's laugh, a spouse's smile and happiness from bonding time. May you receive what touches your heart in a way that you will forever cherish it. For those who are serving or those who are home waiting for them to return I give my most heartfelt Merry Christmas to you. Know that even though you are away you are missed, cherished and most importantly wanted home. Be safe my Airmen, Marine, Sailor and Soldier you will be home before you know it. I salute you! Merry Christmas to all my friends around the world.

Dec 25, 2013

2013 "See Ya" Thought: As 2013 ends I want to say Thank You to those who have made me a stronger person both mentally and physically. My wife and sons continue to inspire me to try and find the path to my success as well as their success. I am reminded that it isn't how much I have in the bank (trust me ain't much) or own that brings me the true joys of life. It is the honest moments we share with and for each other that bring the most reward. As we depart another year take the time to remember all the lessons life has shown you both good and bad because it is In them we find growth. I want to always remember my brothers and sisters in the Armed Forces who continue to inspire me to not waste the freedom I have and the life I can obtain because of their sacrifices. I appreciate all my friends who are always there even when we haven't spoken in a long time. My new Zumba family that always support the "Big Guy" each and every day as I try to pretend to be one of them. Thank You Ladies!

2013 also saw my Navy family see a fellow sailor suffer a traumatic injury to which he will be a vegetable for the rest of his life. His family has faith in their God and support from all of us. Their resolve has reminded me that life is a gift with a hefty price of death at the end of it. It is up to us to cherish that gift each and every day through the way we bring our piece of the pie to society's table. And in this I am grateful for all those who have told me how much I have touched them either through my "Sean's Thoughts" or from the advice I have given over the year(s). The fact that you listen and trust in my words/opinion is a gift that I cannot, with a million words, express the value of to me. My end of 2013 message to you all is "Thanks" because no matter how hard it was or how devastating it may have been to you personally, financially, emotionally or any other "ally" word it is the only year that has made you what you are today....Wiser and stronger. Let's make 2014 a year of rebirth to humanity but before we do let us simply appreciate that we had a 2013. Happy New Year my friends! Be Safe, Be Smart and most of all Be Something Greater than You were Yesterday. Just a thought my friends.
Dec 31, 2013

As we have just passed the birthday of Dr. Martin Luther King I found myself wondering a few things. What would he think of his "Dream" now if he were alive? What would he think of the young men, especially Black/African American, of today? Would he be proud of what he sees before him or would he be ashamed? As I thought about it over the past few days something hit me. First it was subtle in the scope of a whisper deep of a cliff into the jungle below. Then it became louder like the steps of boots creaking across the floor of an old house. Finally it hit me like a car being t-boned by another car that just ran a red light. "I'm Sorry" was the thing that hit me. The words pounded like drums at the Battle of the Bands of the famed Black Colleges of the South. "I'm Sorry!" It didn't ring from some far off place but from deep within my own heart and soul. I thought about Dr. King, President Lincoln, Malcolm X, President Kennedy and all the others who fought for civil rights and equality by giving so much up including their lives.

Where have we come since the bullet that plowed through Lincoln's head? What have we done in the wake of bullets that silenced Malcolm and derailed Kennedy? How have we moved forward with the dream ever since the metal jacket left its snug home of that weapon to find the peace loving civil rights leader Dr. King? The answer is we have gone backwards as a people, a society and a nation. My community, the Black community, once proudly stood having the strongest of mothers who raised men who put their women, children and problems on their backs to be better, find better and do better than those before us. These men didn't want handouts or pity just a chance to stand next to other men as equals. Today's men (in general), of all races, now rather have SWAG and a bunch of expensive cars and bling rather than uplift their image through hard work, commitment and honor. They rather have a bunch of "bitches" and "Babies mommas" than a woman to walk side by side with teaching their children how to be strong, honest, humble but most of all to be a "PART" of society as a whole. The Ladies want thugs and guys with said SWAG that they can have all these babies with but would scoff at a man who wants more than that out himself and his mate.

All the communities be it Black, White, Hispanic, Asian and all parts in between have failed in the Dr. Kings "Dream." Our society isn't free as he had dreamed but it is enslaved by the very thing he and all the others that fought with him thought would save us, Freedom. Our freedom to be whatever we want and act however we want has turned us not into brothers and sisters but into wild animals growling and snarling over the last piece of meat or WIFI as we would have it today. "I'm Sorry!" That

we, as a people and nation, have failed to uphold our end of the bargain and hold each other accountable for our actions and raise each other up for our successes. Dr. King lost his life in the hopes that we would find a way to move forward as "One Nation under God…" and no it does not matter which God you believe in or don't believe in. What matters is that we stood as "one." Dr. King's Dream is not dead but it is in ICU and it is struggling to survive. Every race has people screaming about their "Pride" but very few of them understand what it really means to have earned that very pride. It is time to actually stand up for one another and to praise one another not in the false ways we have grown accustomed to be in the honest ways of getting to know each other and having a person's word be all that is needed. Trust, Honest, Humanity, Brother/Sisterhood and Community are what the "Dream" is about….. Maybe we all need to go back to sleep and find that Dream. Until then…. I am Sorry we are failing to live the Dream! Just a thought my friends.
Jan 21, 2014

What better way to start the famed Black History month than with an epic battle of good vs evil? Yesterday the Twittersphere blew up with the news that saintly rapper DMX will have a celebrity boxing match against the White Devil George Zimmerman (Hopefully you know he is HISPANIC). The ethnic (not just black) community is in celebration of the inevitable beat down that George is about to take. But as usual I was struck with a different thought than the elation of the masses. Is the enemy of my enemy my friend? Would I still keep a clean soul if I ask the devil to take care of those who had done me wrong? I ask these questions because the "community" is behind a guy who made his fortune on exploiting and killing, both directly and indirectly if you believe rap songs, dozens or hundreds of Trayvons. I happen to be a fan of DMX (have all his CD's) but how can we honestly celebrate the death of one 16-year old black innocent kid while ignoring the very fabric of all the innocent 16-year old black and Hispanic kids on the street from the DMX's of the world? How does the savior of the soul of Trayvon become a person who, if you believe his raps, has lived off the very souls of many Trayvons? Celebrating a wrong with another wrong does not make us better. It makes us wrong. As Black History month is upon us I challenge people to understand the sacrifices of the men of the 54th Massachusetts Infantry, The Tuskegee Airmen, The Freedmen and the many men and woman who stood for equality of all people and races. We cannot be so blinded by our overwhelming ignorance of self-diluted value that we forget the reason so many fought for more than they are or could of have been. If "justice" is what we want then let us start in the mirror and teach these young African-American men about the pride of those men mentioned above. That SWAG is nothing but fool's gold designed to keep fools in a state of mental entrapment. The real battle of Good vs Evil is the honor of men and women to carry on the sacrifices that were passed down through blood, sweat, tears and death. Let us begin to pick each other up and fight for righteous things that bring us forward as not only a black community but a world community. Black (or any) History is about pride of where people have come from to attain what they have today. Celebrating DMX vs Zimmerman shouldn't make any community "proud". Just another way to prove that fools will keep themselves down at every opportunity they are given to do so. Just a thought my friends. Now let the fight begin. SMH

Feb 6, 2014

Ladies, if you are tired of getting the same deadbeat douche-bag guys maybe it's time for a wardrobe change. Dress (and act) for the man you want, not the man you are getting. If you want a quality man then be a woman worth the quality of that man. We don't treat a Bentley like a Yugo. Are you a Bentley or a Yugo? Just a thought.
Feb 12, 2014

If you really want to find Happiness the very first and most important step is to be authentically happy with yourself. Happiness starts within and then is projected outwards. Then others will know the real you. Are you happy or are you pretending? Just a thought.
Feb 21, 2014

The more you search for happiness in possessions, other people or other outside sources the further away from it you shall travel. Happiness has to start within the heart and mind of yourself and then be accentuated by the things and people that surround you. Many people have lots of things, lots of friends and even lots of money but have little comfort in their own skin. If you really want happiness I suggest starting on the inside of yourself. Just a thought my friends.
Mar 18, 2014

If people took one step back and tried to see what the other person was saying from the other person's point of view BEFORE reacting, 90% of all conflicts would not exist. Don't bring past bias, ignorance, know-it-all(ness) and judgement to the table of discussion and understanding. All that is needed is open ears, a willingness to understand and a desire to "share" your point of view without the need to "prove" it. Communication starts with listening not with talking! Just a thought my friends.
Apr 4, 2014

Memorial Day Thought: A friend of mine posted a thought remembering those who have fallen defending this nation. In response a friend of his "thanked" him for his service in which he replied "I didn't pay the ultimate sacrifice! I simply partook." I sat with that for awhile and realized something very important. Memorial Day is about the men and women who took their last breath on the battlefield, the oceans deep or the blue skies over the land. It is about those whose bodies were never found and those whose bodies made the long solemn journey home under a flag draped coffin. Yes, Memorial Day is about the legacy of the United States Military member who wrote the check and paid up when the "balance was due." Memorial Day is also for those who didn't pay the ultimate sacrifice but sacrificed nonetheless. It is for every military member that has woken up in the middle of the night because they thought rounds were coming in. For every one who jumps into a defensive posture when something scares them. It is for those who held a comrade as he/she lay in blood wishing he/she could just "go home" knowing he/she is about to die. It is for those who come back home and never make it back to "normal" life. It is for those who could no longer take it and tragically take their own lives to end the noise, the hurt, the pain, the dreams and the fear. No, my friend was wrong he didn't simply "partake" he, like millions of others, sacrificed a lot for our freedoms. So this Memorial Day I say Thank You to all those who paid the ultimate price and all those who stood up and said they would too. Be Safe, Be Smart but most of all Be Appreciative of what that flag really means to those who serve it. Just a thought my friends.

Mar 24, 2014

I was thinking about the death of Dr Maya Angelou and the reaction to it from people all over the internet. As I read all the posts and shared memes about her impact on society, I began to think of Dr. King, Malcolm X, Mother Teresa, Aristotle, Buddha, Jesus and all the thousands of others who tried to lead, educate and improve, not only their communities, but the human species as a whole. Then I realized that in our society today these people would be nothing because we , as people, no longer search for and/or promote the greater good of humanity. Instead we search for how "I" can get all I can get with as little effort as possible.

How would we receive the teachings of those from yesteryear today? Dr. King's "I have a dream" speech would be simply another preacher talking that more people would stand in protest rather than listen to the message it delivered. Our communication has turned from talking to one another to simple text or memes on one of the many social media sites. We allow media to dictate what we care about and allow them to create the outrage that sparks millions to action for the wrong thing, only to move on to the next outrage a day or two later. We have gone from creators of "anything is possible" to followers of "anything that is said or appears on TV." I wonder how far down will we crash as things like respect, integrity, honesty, humility and honor continue to be pushed further and further into the back of our minds.

Our children are created out of need of attention rather than love. They are medicated and placated instead of educated in both scholarly ways and worldly ways. Parenting today is nothing more than keeping kids "distracted" with electronics or some other thing to keep them quiet. If they do not have respect for their parents, a work ethic, or personal strength and understanding, then how can we expect them to be the new leaders? How will we create the great voices of wisdom and triumph when we are unable to stop and listen or articulate a thought past a funny picture with some saying on it. Will Grumpy Cat be our next Dr. King? Sounds funny to ask but the truth is we are headed to just that type of existence.

Dr. Maya Angelou died a week ago, and after 2 days she barely existed. This is the shameful truth of our legacy as we try to get insurance at "half the time" of 15 minutes. The weeds of stupidity have taken control and the wise that would guide us are dying. If Jesus came back today he would probably be laughed off the block and his "flock" would be nothing more than a crazy few. If Buddha shared his wisdom today he would be committed to an asylum. So today my question, friends, is this: Is it too late to turn this ship around or are we destined to ride it over the waterfall to our own destruction? Just a thought, my friends.
Jun 5, 2014

Father's Day Thought: Happy Father's day to the men who raise their sons to be men and their daughters to be women. To the fathers who have to watch their kids grow from a distance and never get to spend time with their children. To the Fathers who raise their kids on their own and yet never makes about anyone else but the children. To the Fathers who have to cry when they are alone because they have to be strong for their family at all times. To the Fathers who are serving in the armed forces all around the world who have pictures of their kids in uniform pockets, taped to vehicle/airplane panels, bunks and computer screens, just to remind them of the gift they have at home. Lastly, Happy Father's Day to my fathers who have guided me to be the man I am today. If it wasn't for you I would not be able to see my two sons grow into bright, intelligent and respectful young men. Thank You from the bottom of my being. Please note I did not say Happy Father's day to the "women" who are being "both daddy and mommy" because frankly that is not only weak minded it is also a desperate attempt for attention. They can be the greatest mom ever but that is what they are: "a mother." A woman cannot be a Father so please let us stop that nonsense and be strong enough to simply allow men to have their day. Happy Father's Day!
Jun 15, 2014

You can scream, yell, post, submit, exclaim and simple tell everyone in the world what a great parent you are till your face turns blue. However, just like school, the grade of your parenting is reflected in the adults you raised. Not every child will find success or the right path no matter what a parent does to raise them "right." That being said, too many kids have no respect for their parents, no sense of discipline, and no understanding of ownership of their actions. These will be the same kids who turn into the young adults we see infesting our world today. To make responsible, respectful and self-assured adults, we must start when they are kids. The "child" is the test and the "adult" is the report card. How's your course going? Just a thought my friends.
Jun 17, 2014

When the "image" of you becomes less important than the "substance" of you a world of happiness will open to you. Too many people spend much of their time trying to prove a title such as Christian, Father, Mother, Boss, Friend, Yogi, Gangster (still a stupid one), Hard, etc., etc., etc. that they continuously find themselves unhappy with life, their station in life and themselves. The title that should matter the most is "me" if you are unable to be true in your own skin, in your own eyes and in your own way you will never fully be free to enjoy happiness. What "images" are holding you back? Just a thought my friends. Jun 29, 2014

I watch people do all this stuff to make themselves look better on the outside. They lift weights, do "the crazy wrap thing", have body cleanses, do all sorts of diet programs, take supplements/pills/roids etc., tan, run, swim and so on and so on and so on. We spend hours upon hours trying to get the outside to look magnificent for whatever reason we have chosen. For all the hard work we do for the outside we do the opposite for the inside. Many people spend their days trying to numb away the world by smoking weed, drinking, pill popping and things of that nature. What good is a car that looks great but has a trashy engine and interior? At the end of the day it doesn't matter if your breasts are huge, your biceps are bulging, your 6-pack is rock hard, your tan is amazing, your hair is perfect, your teeth are whiter than the purity, if you are damaged goods on the inside. If your insides are trash the outside is merely a shell that houses crap. Some people really need a mirror to see what is really going on. How's your insides? Just a thought my friends.

July 10, 2014

The lie(s) you live today will be the crumbling wall you get buried under tomorrow. Your words/actions are the building blocks of the house that becomes you. Every lie or facade you have is a block made of shoddy material that will, not if, fail and crumble. Truth to one's self is the only way to build a stronger you that can withstand the winds of change, destruction and pain associated with emotional growth. So, when you look into the mirror do you believe what you see or do you see a building that is ready to crumble? Just a thought my friends.

July 22, 2014

9/11 Thought: In the moments, days, weeks, months and even years after a tragedy the screams, shock, pain, disbelief, anger and hurt still runs through the soul as if it just happened. Then, as they say, "Time heals all wounds" and we begin to think of it less and less until it is nothing more than a whisper told by those old enough to say, "I was there when it happened." We do not have to look far for the examples of such fading memories. Look at the old man in his Vietnam Veterans hat adorned with his Army Sergeant pin and unit patches. The echoes of the war booming in his fading mind while the youth of today only see an old man holding onto past glory. We forget the pain that was caused by Timothy McVeigh as the building came tumbling down. We forget the echoes of the Kobar Towers in Saudi Arabia from one suspicious truck parked outside. We no longer hear the screams of the mothers who got the news their sons had died on a distant field in France fighting the Germans nor do we truly remember the stench of burning flesh from the many Nazi camps. Even in my hometown of Los Angeles the riots of Watts ('65) and then LA ('92) are distant memories only spoken about if it happens to come up.

Yes, the gift of human kind is that we can carry on to the next day. We can move onto the newest and greatest thing to distract us from our past pains. This gift is also our curse because we forget. Twenty years from now history will say that on this day, like the bombing of the Olympic Village, something horrific happened to innocent people. They will see the pictures of 2 buildings burning with bright red and orange flames and thick black smoke across that perfect blue sky. They will see the pictures and even video of the collapsing of those massive structures and feel the chills of the sound of twisting metal. They will see the faces covered in ash and blood as survivors, first responders and others who just happened to be there climb out of the destruction. Yes, they will learn about it the same way I, as a young boy, learned about Pearl Harbor. They will learn it as just another event that shaped history. And just like with Pearl Harbor it will be something that will not be understood.

Today, however, I'll remember being woken by my mother saying. "Sean, are you alright?" and not knowing what she was talking about. I'll remember turning on the news, as she instructed, and seeing the second plane hit and I'll remember my words "what the fuck!" as I watched. I'll remember getting the phone call from my NCOIC that we were all being recalled immediately and I'll remember Col Dahl's message of "we need to be ready cause we are probably going to war." I'll remember being in Iraq in 2003 and Afghanistan in 2010. I'll remember the loss of MSgt Auckman and SPC Poulin from my units as well as thousands of others from this War on Terrorism. I'll remember all the Wounded Warriors, both physically and mentally injured, who have constant reminders every day of this day that started it all.

One day, I will be an old guy with a cap on for a war long forgotten but not today. Today, I remember the men, women and children who have lost someone or something because of this day 13 years ago. May we never forget the pain we felt when our lives changed. To all my brothers and sisters in the Armed Forces..... Thank You! I'll never forget.
Sept 11, 2014

That awkward moment when you just blew up a public toilet and are walking out of the stall as someone enters the bathroom getting hit in the face with your stench and you make eye contact.
Sept 26, 2014

Today can either be a good day or a bad day..... The choice is yours and yours alone. What type of day will you have? More importantly, what type of day will your bring to those around you? Have a great day, my friends.
Sept 30, 2014

Be careful of the sword of contempt and condemnation that you are wielding in defense of what you believe in because in the end your actions may be worse than those you are condemning. The great "givers" of our past from Jesus to Buddha, from Gandhi to Dr. King and all the little known helpers and educators along the way have given and educated with the backing of "love" not "hate." If you spread your message backed by hate then your message will not only fall on deaf ears but will also consume you in such a way that you are unable to see any other perspective but your own. The questions that arise are this: Are you consumed by the hate to send your message or are you freed by the light of it? Perspective means a lot my friends. May you find the truth in yours. Be easy my friends! Just a thought.

Nov 2, 2014

Veteran's Day Thought: I am a Veteran, no, I am a Combat Veteran. My brave gene is no more prominent than the next person. My fear reactions are just like everyone else's. I have no desire to die or lose a limb in a foreign country while my family sits and worries if I will come home again. I do not want to get up in the morning and put on a uniform nor do I want to sit out in the freezing cold or blistering heat covered from head to toe just to "stand watch." I am no different than the next person with one exception: I AM a Veteran!

I made a promise to the other men and women in uniform that I will stand no matter how deep my fear may boil. I will run into the fire to bring them home with every last breath I have to give. I will stay up all day and all night if it means the men and women under my command/control get to make one more morale call or Skype call to their loved ones.

I made a promise that no matter the destination, the job to be done, the insurmountable odds against us that I will defend not just the Constitution of the United States but also my brothers and sisters in arms across the services. And I will do this knowing that the sounds of bombs going off never stop in the vivid memories. That the images of a fallen soldier in your command lying in a hospital bed on life support for the single reason of letting the family meet the body in order to pull the plug and say goodbye will always be in your mind's eye. That the sound of the boots stomping down in rhythm as yet another flag draped stainless steel coffin is loaded on the back of a C17 or C130 will forever fill me with both joy and sadness so deep that writing about makes me tear up. I will fight on knowing that my spouse will have to wake me up carefully for the rest of our lives because the "combat switch" never gets fully turned off and I may react to being startled. I am a veteran because I know the dangers of the life I chose, I know fear of the impossible unknown and I know the sick stench of death that travels with all of us in uniform to every hostile environment. I shall never be the same person as I was because I AM A VETERAN!

May we never forget that the war(s) rage on for so many who have served and that today is not just about being proud of their sacrifices but also about letting them know we are here for them. Every Combat Veteran has stories that they never share but live over and over and over again in their minds and some of those vets get hooked on drugs, find depression and some tragically take their own life. Let us remember those who have gone before us and served with honor, integrity and pride of the services. In the same breath let us not forget those who are coming home changed forever by a life that can be both amazing and deadly.

To all my Veterans former, current and future I say Thank You for writing that check, living that movie and giving everything you have to make sure that your fellow Soldiers, Marines, Airmen and Shipmates come home. Be Safe, Be Strong, Be Honest and most of all Be Proud because you ARE a VETERAN! Happy Veteran's Day! Now it is time to personally thank every Veteran on my friends list because it's the least I could do. What will you do? Just a thought my friends!
Nov 10, 2014

Apparently I have been too silent so here goes my thoughts: Hate is a parasite that can only live on contempt, misunderstanding, labels of "right" and other hate. All I see and hear from all sides is "hate." I may go deeper into a Sean's Thought soon but right now I'm disappointed at all the hate we, the people, of ALL races, are fueling.
Nov 26, 2014

Thanksgiving Thought: Today is a time to reflect on the things that we are grateful for and the people we are blessed to have in our lives. Today is about our humanity and our love for one another. It is about family and friends, about food and laughter, about old family traditions and new family stories that become tradition. It is about having the first celebration as a newlywed, or newly engaged, or a new parent. It is about the smells of a long passed grandmother's special stuffing recipe slowly cooking as she would say, "just the right way to be perfect" on the stove. It is about arguing over old rivalries in sports until someone comes in and tells you to keep it down. It is about sneaking around the wife just to steal a "little" piece of food and then nearly dying from the blow to the hand you get from her spoon. Thanksgiving isn't about what happened to the Native Americans but what the Native Americans did for the Pilgrims who were dying and in need of humanity. It isn't about getting a 70" TV at 50% off it is about giving a hot plate to a homeless person who no longer can find a smile.

On this Thanksgiving I am grateful for a wife (Keziah) who loves me even through all my pain-in-the-butt flaws, two sons (Sean and Trae) who reflect their parents with honor, intelligence, and an all-around genuine love for people and animals, three mothers (Wanda, Edwina and Kathy) and two fathers (Robert and Woody) who support me in my adventures while always guiding me as parental figures when I seem to go astray. I am grateful to friends who have crawled out of the pits of darkness to bring light to others, friends who change their plans to go to Zumba with me just cause I am in town, friends who don't mind a random 6 a.m. text from me just because I wanted to say hi, friends who bring a smile to my life, my soul and my heart. I am Thankful.

Lastly, I am Thankful for every holiday that I put on a uniform, walked across some crappy ground to a chow hall/DFAC to be greeted by a smiling face of senior leadership and an amazing reminder of home with decorations and foods of all kinds. I am Thankful to the men and women of our Armed Forces who are sitting in one of those places right now laughing and watching whatever sports AFN happens to have on the TV while having a gun on their hip and probably one at their feet. I am Thankful for all the times I spent in that very situation because that is what Thanksgiving is about being grateful for what we are blessed to be a part of in our daily lives. Happy Thanksgiving to each and all of you! May you remember that color does not make a person, God of choice does not make you Godly, Beliefs do not make you right and Hate does not make you strong. Let us stand together as one, understand each other's beliefs while respecting a difference of opinion and find that Love is a much, much, much better vessel to unity. Just a thought my friends! Let's get fat together!
Nov 27, 2014

I often wonder if people really understand what it means to "support" our troops. I hear it all the time. I see it in memes of all sorts with thousands of "likes." I see it in stores who give military discounts and one special days like Veteran's day. So, yes, I see the support and for me I appreciate it. However, what about those who have truly long passed their pride days? Those men and women walking around ever so slowly with only a hat, a pin, a bumper sticker or license plate that reminds us all of their life so long ago? The survivors of the World Wars, Vietnam War and other conflicts long forgotten? How do we support those "troops?"

Today, 73-years ago was (until September 11, 2001) the greatest attack on US soil. The Japanese bombed Pearl Harbor. Those that know me already know how deeply standing in the Arizona Memorial affected me. The voices, the presence, the hurt, the determination, the fight, the will to survive, the brother/sisterhood and the tragedy/triumph of it all coursed through my veins. The truth of life is that we forget those who are too old and frail to remember the sacrifices of sacrifices that have long simmered into casual mention. So, today I am going to "support" our troops by not letting their sacrifices die. Maybe, just maybe, someone who reads what I am saying will take a moment out of their own day to really Thank these men and women who can no longer live on the valor of battles long forgotten. May we all remember and understand that the day we forget those who carried our burdens is the day that burden will return to be carried out again. "If we do not learn from our history we are destined to repeat it." I don't know who said that quote but it is profound indeed. Let us remember the men and women who died from an ambush attack on this day 73 years ago. To all my military friends of present and all those of the past I say Thank You! Sacrifices will live on because some of us refuse to allow them to die. Just a thought my friends.

Dec 7, 2014

As I read all the Facebook messages on "President Dictator", "Illegals", "Muslim", "Christ and Christmas", "Police and racism" etc., etc., etc., etc., etc. I got to thinking about the word "AMERICAN." This is a land that was designed, in theory, since our Founding Fathers actually excluded everyone but their kind initially, to allow people from all walks of life a chance at a dream. No matter if you were devout Christian, Atheist, Scholar, Artist, Muslim, Buddhist, Deaf, Mute, Straight, Gay and all other titles we label ourselves with you were welcome. The only caveat was you must obey the laws of the land. No one person's rights should trump another person's. And though our ancestors were flawed they worked towards that understanding of "if you came in and did things the right way then you could call yourself an American." So many people have forgotten what it means to embrace differences and learn from others. To police ourselves and ensure the scourge are punished not protected and damn sure not allowed to start us rioting (such stupidity). I have been quiet over the last few weeks about what's going on in the world simply because I'm not so sure it is worth commenting on any longer.

That was until Yesterday.

Yesterday, Dec 19, 2014 my dear friend and her husband found their dream of becoming Americans. A little woman

from Chihuahua, Mexico busted her butt and did all the things it took to become a citizen of this great country. The smile on her face (and her husband) reminded me of the ideals that we, as a country, are supposed to embrace and promote. People doing things the right way to gain what they have earned not free handouts for people who are breaking the law be it illegal immigrants, criminals of both the low-life variety and the power suit variety. I am proud to see this family find their place in our dream. More importantly I am proud that her family story reminded me that we must never allow personal pride, agendas, and misinformation to cloud what is fundamentally right for the PEOPLE of the United States of America! Welcome to two very special new Americans. May you both see a better one as we all move forward to being better people. Just a thought!
Dec 20, 2014

Christmas Thought: First and foremost Merry Christmas to all our family and friends who have helped Keziah, Trae, Little Sean and I grow as people this year. May you all find exactly what you need and a couple things you really wanted under the tree. Secondly, Merry Christmas and Happy Holidays to everyone else no matter what you believe in or follow our family wishes you the best today and in the days coming. Thirdly and very humbly, Merry Christmas to all the men and women who are deployed on the ground, in the air, on the sea and under the sea (Navy Subs, you know) who are not able to see their loved one's open presents in person. I wish each and everyone of you a safe deployment and Thank You for your service and sacrifices. I could never say Thank You enough to you all. Fourthly, Merry Christmas to the men, women and families of the Police Departments around the country especially those two NY Police officers executed doing their jobs. In a time where we are suppose to be reflective, appreciative and giving, the seeds of hate have grown and turned into the uncontrollable fires of ignorance and misunderstanding instead of growth and improvement. May we all take the time to see the sacrifices First Responders give on a daily basis while dealing with some of the worst people, places and situations imaginable. May all of you continue to have the strength to do what is right even when it feels pointless. Lastly and most important of all, Merry Christmas to all the men and women of the Armed forces who are struggling with life back home. Suicide is the worst tool given to the world and unfortunately one that is used too often by men and women who gave their all to defend this nation. From the very bottom of my heart and from 22 years of service to this nation I say to each of you, "You are strong enough to stand up out of the darkness and once again fight for the light to carry on, you are NOT alone!" May you (whoever you are, wherever you are) take the time to reach out and get the help because we never leave a man/woman behind.

Special Thank You to everyone that has read my thoughts and have commented on them your support has been one of my most prized gifts. From the Brown's to you, Merry Christmas, Happy Holidays, Happy Hanukkah, Happy Bodhi Day, Happy Kwanzaa and all celebrations I may have missed to you all! Just a Thought my friends.
Dec 24, 2014

CLOSING

So there you have it the random thoughts I had over the course of four years. The imagery, the chaos, the love, the hurt, the pain, the too many "the" in a sentence and the honesty. Very few had been altered from their original posting and all are, for better or worse, something to make us think. So did you? Did you find that one thought that made you stop and think? Did you spend time wondering what the heck this crazy writer is trying to say anyway? Did you find a pathway to childhood memories that made you smile or made you sad? In short, did my journey take you on a journey? I ask these questions because every message, every opinion, every thought we have or share with the world be it via text, social media, over the phone or in person has a potential to change a life, to validate a belief, to challenge a belief, the change an understanding, to create an understanding and even create confusion and conflict. Where did these passages take you on your journey or, better yet, where did you take these passages? With that in mind I challenge you to take a second journey.

Now that you have read it all, pondered the meanings, nodded in agreement, shook your head in disagreement, applauded and scolded these messages and thoughts I ask you to do it again. Go back through but this time sit with one and think about it, digest it, take it to a friend and converse on it and define it for you. No, this isn't about agreeing with my opinions or points but simply challenging your own way of thinking for not only what you don't know and feel but for what you do know and feel about the subjects at hand. I challenge you like I challenge myself to sit again and this time just explore what the message means to you, your friends, your family, your loved ones and the strangers you come across in life. If you are lucky you may find a new path to take on your own journey. Only you can decide that because we all have our own story to live and tell. Speaking of which, I have also been changed.

Yes, working with my dear friend April I had to go through these thoughts one by one. We discussed what she thought as a first time reader of the message. We discussed what I thought hearing it again and then we simply talked if the discussion led us that way. These conversations were both amazing and uncomfortable, as we had to talk about our own personal beings in order to honestly bring a book that has integrity to the writer and the message being delivered. What few people know is that I never (or hardly ever) read my thoughts after they were published on social media. In fact, I often sat down and wrote them that day i posted them. They had grammatical and spelling errors (which we tried desperately to fix) and some were even simply confusing. However, for the most part the thoughts lived as they were and I stayed with them as long as there had been people responding to the posting that, I in turn, responded to each of them.

I tell you all that to say that hearing my words again, this time in April's voice changed it from being something I wrote to something that was being taught to me. I found myself agreeing or disagreeing with the message of the premise of certain messages even though at the time I wrote them the sentiment was authentic, real and raw. I found with some that I would think, "man I could re-post this today and it would still apply." That made me both happy and sad because if it is a 2010 message that can still apply in 2017 then we may have not grown as a people or a nation after all. On the flip side the idea that something I wrote in 2010 that still applies today (that is a good message) reminds me that a truth of life is often timeless. I listened and talked about everything I wrote as a thought over the course of four years. I am forever grateful that I did because this book isn't just for you the reader but it's for me the writer who does not want to forget the very lessons I, as a maturing (OK, maybe not that mature) adult, had learned and wanted to share with others. That being said, I am not the only one who took this adventure. I wanted April to write what this journey has meant or done for her. Maybe her message will help put words to one of your thoughts.

***

April's Message

When Sean first asked me to work with him on this book, I wasn't entirely sure what to expect. What I knew was that he had been writing his thoughts on social media for several years, and that the people that had come in and out of his life, people who were profoundly affected by the messages and conversations, encouraged him to collect his ideas and share them. What I also understood was that writing is a personal and vulnerable act. I could not imagine why this person who I had only met months earlier was asking me to be a part of this. What did he expect from our partnership? What did he hope to accomplish with this book? Why me? Why now?

Sean and I, by some accounts, make an unlikely partnership. At the time, I was on summer break from teaching literature and writing at the local high school, and enjoying a fairly comfortable life in our small town in western Washington. As Sean would tell it, he was just a group fitness instructor. However, what is shrouded in that minimalist description is the truth: he is more than that. He had become, in a very short period of time, a dear friend and confidante. As I read hundreds of my friend's thoughts, I realized that, though I was, in a small way, helping Sean achieve a dream, he was, in a much larger way, impacting the way I thought, the things I believed, the values that defined who I was.

We had previously spent many hours discussing everything from politics to parenting, from religion to relationships, from fidelity to social facades. It was during these discussions I realized something that would define our conversations and ultimately our work on this book:

256

Sean has an uncanny way of challenging the facades I had constructed to craft what appeared to be an ideal life. The trouble with ideal is that it, too, is a facade. It was through these conversations that I started to examine long- held assumptions and beliefs about life, the world, myself. For a person who generally considers herself rational and intelligent, (ok, a bit controlling) acknowledging that these fundamentals might be in need of examination made me, well, uneasy. However, on some level I knew that that was exactly what drew me to this friendship; it was exactly what I had been looking for, for longer than I was eager to admit. So, when Sean asked me to help with the book, there was no hesitation.

Over the course of several weeks, I read, reflected on, and responded to each individual thought. I struggled in the beginning with how I should read this. Should I read as the teacher, critic, friend, or something else? As a result, my initial responses were disjointed. I began searching for patterns and connections among the thoughts, trying to understand my friend and his work. In the writing, I found the voices of a philosopher, patriot, lover, father, and several other distinct personas. As I read, I found searching for patterns, while an important part of my experience, were limiting my ability to just be in the moment with each message. I needed to find balance in this process.

Throughout this, Sean reminded me to read authentically for myself. To be honest, I sometimes wondered what that meant? The answer eventually came when I started to shift my focus from understanding the writer, to trying to understand my own reactions as a reader. There were thoughts that I read for which I had no response. Not that the ideas had no value. Rather the messages aligned with my own thinking or sparked little reaction. On the other hand, sometimes I didn't respond for the opposite reason: the ideas affected me so strongly that I couldn't formulate a response that would capture the feelings and thoughts I was having. Then there were thoughts that, frankly, knocked the breath out of me. These thoughts challenged assumptions I held about my life, my values, my relationships, and my loyalties. It would have been easy to turn the page and move on to a more comfortable thought. However, there was something compelling in the act of bringing the assumptions into the light. This was not at all simple or painless. In fact, it was at times frustrating, unnerving, painful. This was magnified by our conversations as we went through the book, thought by thought, comment by comment.

As I read, I kept asking myself, why would someone read this? What value would they find in another person's musings about life, love, parenting, race, war? I realized the answer was quite simple: the value is in our thinking. Taking an idea and sitting with it, measuring it against what we believe and what we think we know, that's where the value lies. In the thoughts I also found the value of conversation. Conversation? In a book? Yes, in a book. Granted, I had the luxury of talking with Sean at length about his ideas. Getting the backstory and further insight through our discussion. However, I also began sharing some of the thoughts with friends, family, and my students. As a result of sharing the thoughts and the questions they raised, we began to talk differently, openly about relationships, race, bigotry, love, hate, personal responsibility, and truth. The entries became for me a springboard for open and honest dialogue about topics that matter to us. That matters to all of us.

If I had one hope it would be that each person who reads this book take their time, sit with each thought, consider it, measure it, discuss it. In the end, though, I can't tell you how to read this book. I wouldn't want to. The journey has to be your own. But once in awhile, as you take this journey, be sure look up. Or, you might just miss out on something beautiful.

...

My journey's not over. Let it never be over.

Make every word count. What would you do if you only had those few words or a few actions left for your life? Do not waste your time, your very precious time, on hate, self-hate, doubt, negative people, harmful relationships. The next minute of life will not come to someone so embrace what you can and what you love. Take a journey and experience the people, the places and the colors of the world. When that last breath comes let that final memory be filled with love, laughter and adventures. All up to you. Just a thought my friends.

March 8,2017

So here is the thing about writing a book that contains personal thoughts it is hard to find the best way to walk away. As you have seen I did a closing and then added a thought which, in all honesty, could very well be the end but that just wouldn't be me. I simply am not satisfied I am ending this the way my heart says I should end it. That changed when I remembered the caption I wrote with the picture of myself I used for this book. Yes, these words were written by me for each and everyone who reads them. So without further ado I give you the final message of my book.

You don't know me! You don't know what lies behind the eyes and the smiles, the frowns and the tears. You don't know me! You don't know what things I fear most in losing, in battle, in life or in general. You don't know me! You don't know the thoughts I have when the room is quiet and there is no one around to distract my mind. You don't know me! You don't know if I am capable of absolute love or absolute hate or something absolutely in-between. You don't know me! You don't know if my brashness is arrogance or if it is shyness being hidden by a facade to protect the spirit. You don't know me! And you don't have to know me to understand one thing about me that I understand about you. We are all complex creatures with emotions and feelings both rational and irrational. We are all loving and hateful, healing and hurtful, strong and fragile all at the same time. You don't have to know me to sit with me and talk, spend time, enjoy the laughter in the moment, or the tear in the memory. To know me is to not know me at all because, you don't know me and I don't know you. Treat each person as if you want to know more about them and you will forever spend time getting to know them and possibly truly enjoying the ride. You don't know me!

90144210R00146

Made in the USA
Columbia, SC
27 February 2018